How To Predict The Future By Creating It Yourself

The User's Manual For Your Subconscious Mind

CHAD CHESMARK

ISBN-13:978-1983538056
ISBN-10: 1983538051

DEDICATION

To my parents who've always encouraged me to follow my passion, and who were always willing to sit through, "Just one more card trick."

CONTENTS

ACKNOWLEDGMENTS..vii

1 THE BEGINNING..1

2 WHY I WROTE THIS BOOK..9

3 WHO THIS BOOK IS FOR...13

4 THE BACKSTORY...17

5 HOW FAST YOU CAN EXPECT RESULTS....................23

6 USING YOUR MIND TO PREDICT THE FUTURE...................29

7 THE EFFECTIVE WAY TO SET GOALS.......................37

8 THE ART OF LISTENING & LEADERSHIP.................43

9 POWERFUL WORDS & HOW TO USE THEM............46

10 THE MOTION EMOTION CONNECTION................54

11 VISUALIZATION...58

12 THE SECRETS OF HYPNOSIS..................................64

13 THE EXTRAORDINARY POWER OF INTUITION.............85

14 OVERCOMING FEAR..93

15 OWNING THE STAGE: THE POWER OF PUBLIC SPEAKING AND WHY IT'S ESSENTIAL TO YOUR SUCCESS 103

16 TAKE ACTION 126

17 PERSISTENCE.. 133

18 THE POWER OF GRATITUDE 138

19 HOW TO IMPLEMENT EVERYTHING 141

20 NETWORKING 101 143

CONCLUSION 148

FREE BONUS For Buying This Book:

Download the FREE Achievement Action-Plan Workbook
by visiting http://leadershipmindpower.com/workbook/

ACKNOWLEDGMENTS

I want to start by thanking my personal coaches and mentors, Barry Friedman, Anton Zellman, and Richard Barker. I would like to use this medium to thank all of you for pushing me to step out of my comfort zone time and again. Your ability to challenge and encourage me has been an incredible beacon of motivation along my journey. Your continued support and openness to share your insights and experience has meant everything to me. I hope that I am able to share your wisdom and help others in the achievement of their goals, dreams, and desires.

I also want to thank the hundreds of authors who have transformed my life, especially Napoleon Hill, whose life of sharing has opened so many doors for myself and thousands of others. I am so grateful to all of those who took the time to put their thoughts, philosophies, and wisdom on paper to share with the world.

Finally, I'd like to thank my closest friend, James Michael, who taught me how to laugh until it hurts. You're the funniest person that I've ever met, and your influence and friendship mean everything.

Thank you.

1 THE BEGINNING

A grandfather is talking with his grandson and he says there are two wolves inside of us which are always at war with each other. One of them is a good wolf, which represents things like kindness, bravery, love, leadership and taking action. The other is a bad wolf, which represents things like greed, hatred, procrastination and fear. The grandson stops and thinks about it for a second. Then he looks up at his grandfather and says, But Grandfather, which one wins? The grandfather quietly replies, The one you feed. – Unknown

This book is all about feeding that good wolf...with achievement-crushing nourishment.

Introduction

Is it possible to read minds, predict the future, and reach your ultimate destiny? The answer is a big fat YES! If you learn the systems within these pages, and apply the methods explained effectively, you will become the closest thing to a real life mentalist. You will be able to reach any goal, you will become a great leader, and your life will transform in ways that you never dreamed possible.

I realize that I've just made quite a claim, so let me briefly explain how all of this is going to work. Have you ever wondered what it is that separates super-star achievers from average people? What special tools did people like Albert Einstein, Thomas Edison, and Steve Jobs have that others seem to be lacking? Were they lucky? Were they just smarter than everyone else? Or, is there something more to solving this puzzle? It's actually a combination of several things. Sure, Einstein was smarter than most when it came to physics, but he probably wouldn't have been able to duplicate the success that Steve Jobs had with Apple. These people had a unique genius in different fields of expertise. Unless you happen to be obsessed with computers, you probably don't stand a chance at duplicating Job's efforts either. And likewise, Thomas Edison, although he was a master of invention, had no exceptional talent when it came to athletics. Each of their genius existed in a very focused forum.

The good news is that each one of us has our own inner genius. In order to reach the level of a super-star achiever, you'll need to find out what your inner-genius is. Once you know what it is, you can begin to hone it in a way that will lead you to exponential success. But, simply knowing what your inner genius is isn't enough.

The next step, one that every super-star achiever must complete, is to use the entirety of your mind towards enhancing that genius. Most average people, even those who are in their fields of genius, never reach the highest levels of success because their conscious and subconscious minds are not congruent with their goals. Without complete congruence between the two parts of your brain, your conscious mind will be consistently battling a much, much, more powerful subconscious mind. Our subconscious minds do not like change, and they will do everything in their power to thwart our progress.

The most successful people in the world have, either consciously or unconsciously, figured this mind-connection thing out. You've probably heard the story about Thomas Edison and his invention of the light bulb. Edison failed more than 10,000 times before finding a light bulb that actually worked. Without having complete mental focus, both consciously and subconsciously, Edison would have certainly quit before reaching that goal. He was able to become so extremely concentrated on achieving that single goal because both parts of his mind were in complete congruence. When both your conscious and subconscious minds are in congruence, real magic can happen.

Some super-star achievers are able to reach this point of mental congruence on their own, but these people are rare. That's why they're so well known, respected, and remembered. It's as though they were born with a special gift that allowed them to tap into this power at will. For most of us, attaining complete mental focus and establishing congruence between our conscious and subconscious minds is not something that comes naturally. We're never taught how to do it in school. It takes extreme effort and an application of the proper knowledge to succeed at the highest levels. The main purpose of this book is to help you do just that.

In my years of research, I have collected the most effective ways to help you reach a state of complete mental focus that you can apply to almost any goal. I say "almost" any goal, because these principles and techniques will be most effective when applied to your area of inner genius. For example, I could make it my goal to become a linebacker for the Pittsburgh Steelers. Even if I apply all of the techniques in this book for several years, chances are that I will fail miserably. Why? It's probably because I'm over 40 years old, 188 pounds, and not as good at playing football as I'd like to think. Even though I absolutely love football, it is not my genius. My genius is speaking, performing on stages, and helping others to achieve their goals, so I choose to apply these principles to that. No, I didn't just call myself a genius. I'm simply stating where my passion lies.

If you don't know what your inner-genius is, it's time to start thinking about it. What is it that you love to do more than anything else in the world? What topic can you talk about for hours without ever growing tired? Whatever that is, it is probably your inner genius. If your ultimate goal is to make a certain amount of money, the best thing that you can do is to find a way to make that money within your area of genius. Sure, this process will help you achieve any goal that you desire, but its power will be magnified a thousand times if you apply it to something that you're truly passionate about. Something that runs parallel with your inner genius.

Many people have described the principles that you're about to learn as The Law of Attraction. While I champion The Law of Attraction, I find that much of the information out there about the LOA is incomplete. Most of the books, videos, and courses that I've studied concerning the LOA have left out essential steps and end up delivering a watered-down version of the concept. They teach a version that simply does not produce results.

If you apply all of the principles in this book, which will include all of the missing and necessary concepts from The Law of Attraction, you will have everything you need to actually get it working in your life.

My Discovery of This System

Before you completely dive into the material, I want to give you a little information about my background, so that you know where all of this is coming from. I also want to explain how I effectively apply the concepts in this book on a daily basis. If you've never seen me speak or perform, then you've probably never heard of me, so I will first introduce myself.

My name is Chad Chesmark, and I make a living speaking to companies and groups about harnessing the hidden powers of the mind to achieve success through leadership, The Law of Attraction, and self-hypnosis. I personally use the methods in this book to consistently predict the future, read minds, and inspire others. I apply simple techniques, that you will soon be incorporating into your own life, on stages as well as in my personal life. When giving live presentations, I play the role of a mentalist, magician, hypnotist, comedian and motivational speaker. In my programs, I am able to accurately predict the future night after night, and soon, you will do the same in extremely powerful ways.

I do not have any special powers or a psychic sixth-sense. I wasn't abducted by aliens or struck by a lightning bolt. The methods that I use are available to anyone who has a willingness to learn them. Now don't worry, this is not a book about voodoo, witchcraft, or anything that has to do with having supernatural powers. That being said, when you see the results that you're about to generate, in both your professional and personal life, by taking action on the techniques in this book, you just might start to believe in magic.

Over the years, I have been fortunate enough to study under some of the greatest minds in the world. I have done this through multiple personal coaches, seminars, classes, and by way of personal experience. Not to mention absorbing thousands of books. My personal system for achieving your destiny through leadership and self-mastery is a culmination of all that I have learned.

In this book, I will only share the techniques and methods that have proven to be impactful. I was very skeptical when discovering many of techniques outlined in this success system, especially concerning The Law of Attraction, and I'm sure that you will be as well. That's fine. In fact, I welcome skepticism. Don't believe anything that I write in this book on faith. Instead, I urge you to be scientific towards what you're about to learn. Never simply take my word for it. Test the principles for yourself, and when you test them, go all in.

This is not an a-la-carte system where you can choose to try only one or two of the principles. If you're going to give it a go, give it one hundred percent. That is the only way that you'll experience the true power of your subconscious mind, and the true power of destiny building through leadership. That being said, it is quite all right to tackle each step one at a time in order to avoid information overload.

My journey into the subconscious mind began when I was very young. I began studying the art of magic at the age of six when my parents purchased a Mickey Mouse Magic Kit as one of my birthday gifts. Many children have magic as a hobby at some point in their lives, but for most, it passes as they discover other interests. For me, it still hasn't passed. I've spent my entire life reading and studying everything that coincides with magic. This includes psychology, sociology, hypnosis, Neuro-linguistic programing (NLP), showmanship, memory techniques, misdirection, leadership, nonverbal communication, The Law of Attraction, and marketing.

I have found that, when I combine all of these elements with my five natural senses, I am able to do things that most would view as impossible. And these things "appear" to give me a sixth sense. There's nothing paranormal about what you're going to learn in this book. While predicting the future and reading someone's mind, might seem like it would require some special magical gift, it does not. I'm sure that you've heard the quote by Aristotle that states, "The whole is greater than the sum of its parts." For this book, imagine that the 'parts' are your five basic senses combined with the techniques explained throughout. When used together, the 'whole' will equal something much greater, and more powerful, than the individual 'parts.' The greater sum of the "whole" is where the magic happens in The Law of Attraction.

The success and leadership system outlined in this book will not turn you into a psychic. You will not be able to predict the lottery, speak to the dead, heal the sick, or know in advance who will win the Super Bowl. What you WILL learn are techniques and strategies that will make you a better leader to others, and to yourself, in every aspect of your life. You will be able to design the exact future that you want, and then will it to happen. You will create better business and personal relationships, overcome fear, and tap into the most powerful tool at your disposal. That tool is your subconscious mind.

Daily Applications

I currently use the methods explained in this book in all areas of my life. When I perform as a speaker, mentalist, and/or hypnotist, I use them to demonstrate, in a theatrical way, just how much can be accomplished when we put our subconscious minds to work. I show, through a series of seemingly random experiments, how we can shape our destiny when we know exactly what we want that destiny to be.

During my speaking demonstrations, I use every skill at my disposal to accomplish the outcomes that I desire. I demonstrate the power of listening, non-verbal communication, visualization, self-hypnosis and the ability to "predict" the future. The results of these demonstrations are often described by my audience as mind-blowing examples of the end result that leadership and Law of Attraction mastery can attain. If you see my live presentation, and you read this book, you will not be able to recreate my exact demonstrations. That is because I am combing the leadership techniques, and success system, with advanced training in the art of magic, hypnosis, and NLP (Neuro Linguistic Programing). These are skills that took me a lifetime to master in order to accomplish the things that I do on stage. This book isn't specifically about becoming a stage performer or a public speaker, but is instead designed to help you to predict the exact future that YOU desire. The future of YOUR dreams and YOUR inner genius, not mine.

Even though you won't be able to look at a person and know the exact word that he or she is thinking at the moment, as I do in my speaking program, you will be able to apply the techniques in your own way. You will be able to incorporate your own life experiences, knowledge and areas of expertise, in a way that will amplify your success. This book will teach you how to become a better leader and how to create, and reach, your designed destiny. It will not teach you how to be me, a speaker and psychological entertainer, unless that's what you truly desire for your own destiny.

When I'm not demonstrating these principles on stage, I use them to shape my life. I've used them to create my dream career, travel the world, meet the woman of my dreams, stay healthy and physically fit, etc. I have become the person that I am today, not by chance, but by following a plan of action that I have created, using the techniques in this book. Everything positive that I have accomplished in life were born as simple thoughts. I then created action plans, based on a vision of who I wanted to become, and then programed my subconscious mind to become that person. If you don't know who you want to be, then you're just leaving it up to chance. If you leave it up to chance, you might not like who you become. Motivational speaker, Jim Rohn says it like this, "If you don't design your own life plan, chances are you'll fall into someone else's plan. And guess what they have planned for you? Not much."

While I'm happy to be where I'm at today, I have not yet completely fulfilled my vision. The process takes time, and there are many stepping-stones to reach along the way. By having my vision in place, I know that I am on the right track and will continue to grow into the person that I intend to become. This book will show you exactly how to do just that. It will show you how to become the best you that you can envision. You'll most likely find, as I do, that as you come closer to reaching your vision, you'll want to keep on moving the goalpost further and further. When you realize that your plan is working, you'll gain the courage to continually raise the bar, pushing yourself to become an even better version of you than you could have previously imagined. It's like the Aerosmith lyrics that say, "Life's a journey, not a destination." While that is very true, without a destination in mind, you will not get far at all. Let's work together to get you further than you ever thought possible. Sound good?

2 WHY I WROTE THIS BOOK

Those who are unaware they are walking in darkness will never seek the light. - Bruce Lee

Most Are Unaware of Their Full Potential

I wrote this book for several reasons, but the biggest is that it drives me crazy to see people settling for a life of mediocrity. So many of us accept the life that is handed to us by chance. We tend to work at jobs that we don't love, don't live where we truly want to live, and don't do what we're passionate about doing. The majority of the world seems to be walking through life as though they're in the Matrix. They just go with the flow of life. It's like they're floating on a raft in the middle of the ocean, just hoping to end up somewhere that doesn't suck.

Let's assume that this is the only life that we get. I don't know what your spiritual or afterlife beliefs are, but for now, just assume that this is it, and that we only get one shot. Think of how impossible it is that you even exist. How lucky you are to be alive. To live in a time when literally anything is possible. That you don't live in a country where pursuing your dream is difficult or even illegal. When you look at it like that, it should become your duty to become the best you that you can be.

I've met hundreds of people who don't have the opportunities that we have. For seventeen years, I've traveled the world performing my mind reading and hypnosis shows on the nicest cruise ships on the planet. While the ships themselves are magnificent, some of the ports that they explore are not. Sure, the beaches and tours that are designed exclusively for tourists are great, but when you walk through some of these towns, there's nothing to see but poverty. When you see people suffering, stuck in a place where the average monthly salary is less than five dollars, and clean water is a luxury, it can really make you think. For one, it forces you to feel grateful for the opportunities that you have. Opportunities that we otherwise tend to take for granted.

I often perform magic for the beggars that I find on the streets of these ports. I usually do some sleight of hand, magically turn something into money, and then give it to them to keep. It's pretty amazing to see their reactions, because most have never seen a magician before, and the money can be enough to change their life. I'm not talking about a lot of money either. Twenty dollars can equal several months' worth of food for them and their families.

One time, I ended up talking to a young street beggar in Ensenada, Mexico. He believed that everyone in America was wealthy. When I told him that was actually not the case, he was disgusted. He grabbed my arm, which freaked me out a bit, looked me in the eyes and said, "You people don't know how lucky you are. You can do anything you want. Be anything you want to be. So, why doesn't everyone choose to be great?" Good question, and that's exactly what I'm talking about. Too many of us would like to be great, but don't ever consciously choose to be great. Too many people never take action towards becoming extraordinary. That's why I wrote this book. To help more people choose, and achieve, greatness.

The fact that you're reading this book, shows that you're not one of those people who settle for what life decides to hand you. You are someone who knows in your heart that there's more to this life than there seems. You know that the most successful people in the world are no different than you, and you've decided to do something about it. I'm confident that the information in this book, if taken action upon, will help you achieve the life that you desire and deserve.

HOW TO PREDICT THE FUTURE BY CREATING IT YOURSELF

You can get everything in life you want if you will just help
enough other people get why they want- Zig Ziglar

Reaching More People

I know that right now, you're probably thinking, "Ok, Chad. Stop telling me what you're going to share with me and start sharing already." Don't worry. I promise that we'll get to that soon enough, but I first want to lay the foundation, so that we have something to build upon. By first introducing the how, why, what, when, and where, it will help you to better understand the principles that lie ahead. Besides, I want to create a relationship with you before I start giving you a to-do list. I want you to know that this information is coming from a friend and not some random stranger.

Another reason that I decided to write this book is to be able to reach as many people as possible. I can only touch a limited number of people through speaking, but a book's potential outreach is unlimited. I feel that it is my duty to share this information. When you have a set of knowledge that's powerful enough to transform someone's life, it must be shared, especially, if it doesn't cost you anything but time to share it. I know that not everyone who reads this will actually apply the concepts to their lives, but as long as I've put it out there to be discovered, I'll feel that I've done something good for the world.

The skills that I have acquired came from reading hundreds, or even thousands of books, working with coaches and mentors, and from personal experience. What I've done is take everything, from years of study that have actually worked for me, and put them into a single success system. I've left out any techniques that didn't produce results, so what you're getting here is only the stuff that has actually worked for me. I mean for this book to contain enough information, tools, and tactics to help you gain unstoppable momentum toward reaching your destiny. I hope that you continue to read all of the thousands of books written about success and leadership that are out there, but my intent is for this single book to have everything that you need, so as to guide you on your way to achieving greatness.

> The written page is the only way the dead can teach the unborn.
> - Abraham Lincoln

Selfish Reasons For Writing This Book

My final reasons for writing this book are selfish ones. I once heard the magician Penn Jillette, from Penn & Teller, say something like, "If you want to live forever, write a book." By putting all of your thoughts on paper, and then sharing those thoughts with the world, in a sense, you will live forever. The thought of leaving this world, without sharing what I've learned through a lifetime of study, frightens me. Writing this book is my attempt to join the club of immortal authors.

I'm also writing this book for myself. Until now, all of the concepts that I use as a mentalist, speaker, hypnotist, and coach, have existed only in my mind, and in countless, unorganized journals that I've kept over the years. In writing this, I now have a personal resource that I can use to clarify my thoughts and success system. The most difficult thing that you will learn in this book is to be persistent in applying the techniques. It's very easy to know the information, but not apply it. I too suffer from this dilemma from time to time.

Writing everything down will help serve as a reminder to myself, just how powerful these techniques are, and that I must continue to apply them, on a daily basis. Throughout your journey, you will hit plateaus, become complacent, and forget that there's more that you can accomplish. Writing this book is my personal reminder to always keep the momentum moving forward. In life, we are either moving forward or retreating. I aim to always move forward, and hope that you will as well.

3 WHO THIS BOOK IS FOR

If we did all the things we were capable of, we would literally astound ourselves. - Thomas Edison

Anyone Who Knows That They Have More To Offer

This book was written for those who just know, in their gut, that they have untapped potential. Starting today, stop saying to yourself that "someday" you're going to do great things. Someday is today! I want you to make a promise to yourself right now. Take out a piece of paper and write this down: "I promise to try everything that I'm about to read, for the next 21 days, whether I think it will work or not." If you know that you haven't reached your full potential in life, if you know that you haven't fulfilled your destiny, then you owe it to yourself to do something about it. Stop telling yourself that you'll get around to it "someday." Do it now, and don't risk looking back ten years from now, only to think, "I wonder where I'd be if I had committed to really trying that system."

You are far more powerful than you know, and in this book, I'm going to show you how to tap into that power. You see, the problem with the human brain is that we're never given an instructional manual for it. Do you remember the 80's television show, "The Greatest American Hero?" If not, then I just made myself sound really old. Anyway, the show was about a school teacher who received a superhero costume, from aliens, that would give him the powers of flight, superhuman strength, invisibility, super speed, etc. The problem was that he lost the instructions for the costume and had no control over its abilities, so he consistently crashed into buildings and his superpowers were all over the place. He had no instruction on how to focus and control the costume's powers. Our minds are like that costume. We have an unbelievable amount of power in built into our skulls, but most of us don't know how to tap into it. This book will show you how.

We've all seen how powerful a mind can be. Look at people like Albert Einstein, Thomas Edison, Mozart, Michelangelo, and Steve Jobs. What made these people different? Did they have something that you and I don't? No. They were humans, just like us, with brains just like ours. What made them different was their ability to tap into the deeper parts of their mind. You have a genius hiding inside of you. All you have to do is figure out what it is, and how to nurture it. When you find what you're most passionate about, you have found your genius. The next step is to help it grow into its full potential, and to do that, you will need to reprogram your subconscious mind.

Leadership is the capacity to translate vision into reality.
Warren G. Bennis

Those Who Want To Become Better Leaders...And That Means YOU!

In order to create and fulfill your ultimate destiny, you must first become a leader. Why? It's because nothing great is accomplished alone. The techniques in this book can be applied directly to becoming a better leader. I want you to start seeing yourself as a corporation. You are not alone on your journey towards success. You will be too busy, in your pursuit of greatness, to worry about every little detail. You must surround yourself with a team who will help you achieve your goal. This task is impossible without leadership.

Don't take it from me. Look at the great leader, Henry Ford. After WWI, a newspaper published an article claiming that Mr. Ford was ignorant. Ford ended up in court with a libel suit filed against the newspaper. During the hearing, the paper's lawyers asked Mr. Ford a series of questions about historical events, facts and dates. Mr. Ford couldn't answer most of the questions and eventually replied:

> If I should really want to answer the foolish question you have just asked, or any or the other questions you have been asking me, let me remind you that I have a row of electric push-buttons on my desk, and by pushing the right button, I can summon to my aid men who can answer any question I desire to ask concerning the business to which I am devoting most of my efforts. Now, will you kindly tell me, why I should clutter up my mind with general knowledge, for the purpose of being able to answer questions, when I have men around me who can supply any knowledge I require?

If Henry Ford surrounded himself with a team to accomplish his goals, then you should do the same. By reading this book, you will learn powerful techniques that will turn you into a compelling leader, influencer and persuader. You will learn how to motivate others, in mutually beneficial ways, to help you reach your destiny much faster.

Those Interested in The Powers of the Mind

If you're like me, and have a fascination with the powers of the mind, then you will enjoy this book. We're going to explore techniques that the greatest minds of all time have implemented on their road to greatness. We're going to dive into the subconscious mind and learn how to make it work for your benefit. It's been said that we only use 10 percent of our brains. That's technically not true, because science actually shows us that we use 100 percent. In fact, in an article in Scientific America, Robyn Boyd writes, "Ultimately, it's not that we use 10 percent of our brains, merely that we only understand about 10 percent of how it functions." For this book, I want you to think of it in NLP (Neuro-Linguistic Programing) terms. In NLP and hypnosis, it is suggested that 10 percent of our brain represents our conscious mind, and the other 90 percent, our subconscious. For our purposes, this is the ideal explanation. Our aim is to get that 90 percent to be in tune with the 10 percent so that we can take control of our lives.

The good news is that you don't have to know exactly how it works in order to use it effectively. I don't understand how my laptop works, yet I use it every day. I ask you, while reading this, not to worry so much about why these techniques work, and instead focus on the results that they generate. If you're skeptical on the powers of the subconscious mind, I suggest you look into the research done by neuroscientist, David Eaglemen. Eaglemen has a documentary series about the influence that our subconscious, or unconscious minds have on our conscious minds. In it, he states that, "There is debate in the field about whether consciousness even has efficacy." He goes on to describe how our decisions are actually made by our unconscious minds a few seconds before they ever reach our conscious minds.

If what Eaglemen says is true, then it is imperative that we learn how to train our unconscious, or subconscious, minds so that they're working in harmony with what we want our destinies to become. Without the approval of our subconscious minds, it is impossible to achieve greatness. In this book, you will learn how to reprogram your subconscious mind to do whatever you want it to do, and in doing so, you will have a wealth of power at your disposal.

4 THE BACKSTORY

Think & Grow Rich

Some people are able to be successful in life without ever picking up a motivational book, like the one you're reading right now, but not me. If it wasn't for books, coaching, and trial and error, I'm pretty certain I'd be lost. Since learning and applying the leadership and success principles described in this book in my own life, I have come across successful people who have never read a nonfiction book in their lives. How did they become successful if they didn't know these secrets? The truth is that they DO know these secrets. They just don't KNOW that they know them. Some people instinctively do these things, while others need to be taught. I was in the latter group.

I always knew that I wanted to make a living speaking on stage, but had an agreement with my parents, that I could pursue anything that I wanted only after I graduated from college. So, I went to school and earned a degree in public relations, with minors in sociology and theater arts. After graduation, I took a job with a large hardware chain making $25,000 per year. At the time, that seemed like a ton of money to me, so I was thrilled.

The job required me to travel, and live in hotels, Mondays through Fridays. I spent my evenings in Holiday Inns, writing my magic and mind reading show, with the hope of turning professional when I was ready. I was already performing at local comedy clubs and for corporate events on the weekends, but was still only a part-time performer.

Once I managed to save up enough money to survive on for six months, I quit my job. I was only at the "real" job for a single year. I had also purchased a marketing course, specifically designed for speakers and entertainers, for $300. So here I was, a 22-year-old entertainer, still living with my parents, with a monthly living expense of about $1,200. The marketing course said that I should set a weekly income goal, so I decided that $400 a week would do. I realize now that these numbers relatively small, but I was young, naive, and didn't have many bills. Oh, to be young again.

For the first seven months of being a self-employed magician, I managed to reach my weekly goal of $400 zero times. Yes, you read that correctly. Not even once did I book $400 worth of shows in a week's time. I was starting to panic, thinking that I might have to go back to another "real" job. It was at that moment, seven months in, that everything changed.

The "Magic" Book

I was sitting around my parent's house, waiting for someone to call and hire me for a show, while simultaneously reading a biography about the martial artist, Bruce Lee. Bruce had been a childhood hero of mine and had inspired me to study martial arts, a hobby that I still practice today. The book had a quote from Bruce that said something like, "I owe most of my success to the book, 'Think & Grow Rich' by Napoleon Hill." I thought nothing of it at the time, and continued on with my day.

A few days later, I was given another book as a gift from the parents of my girlfriend at the time. The book was "Dirty Jokes and Beer," by comedian, Drew Carey. I leafed through the book and stopped on a random page. The very first thing that I read, was something along the lines of, "I owe most of my success to the book, 'Think & Grow Rich,' by Napoleon Hill." I immediately jumped in my rusty, brown-colored Ford Escort, drove to the nearest bookstore, and purchased the book. There was no Amazon back then, only brick & mortar bookstores, so the 20-minute drive was necessary. Today, I would've instantly downloaded the book. Man, I love technology.

I read "Think & Grow Rich" from cover to cover, in a single day, and decided to give its teachings a try. I promised myself to do absolutely everything that Napoleon Hill had suggested in the book. If the methods failed, I wanted to know that it wasn't because I had skipped a step or two. I also decided to raise my weekly income goal from $400 to $1000. If I was going to fail, I was going to fail big. Shoot for the stars, and you might hit the moon, right?

I wrote down my goals, affirmations, and action plan on small note cards and kept them with me at all times. I vowed to read them, at least twice per day. Once in the morning, as soon as I awakened, and once at night before going to sleep. I also put post-it notes, with my goals written on them, all over the house where I was sure to see them often. I was unknowingly using self-hypnosis techniques, a key point that I wouldn't come to realize until years later. At first, I experienced no results. I was starting to doubt Hill's methods, but after three weeks, something magical happened.

As an entertainer and speaker, I was a self-employed independent contractor and was keeping track of my goals, not by money received, but by events booked. In order to count as being achieved, I had to book at least $1000 worth of magic and speaking gigs each week. At that time, I was only charging a few hundred dollars for an appearance, so reaching my goal meant booking about five per week. Since I had previously failed to book even $400 for a single week prior to reading the book, $1000 seemed impossible. It wasn't. After reading my note cards for three weeks, I finally had my first $1000 week. Then, for fifty-two weeks in a row, I reached my goal every single week. Yes, for an entire year I reached or exceeded my goal every single freaking week! "How was this even possible?", I thought.

The crazy thing was that I wasn't doing anything different, other than reading the cards, than what I had been doing during my first seven months of failure. For some reason, reading those cards twice a day changed everything. I began to get "lucky" all of the time. I always seemed to be in the right place at the right time, meet the people that I needed to meet, and book the exact number of shows that I needed to reach, or sometimes exceed my goal. It was as though I had unlocked a magical door to the universe that would somehow guarantee my success.

I didn't understand why this was working so well, but I certainly knew that it was. Had I discovered some secret formula that would enable me to do anything that I could dream of? Once I realized that such a powerful, effective and mysterious tool existed, I decided to apply the techniques to an even bigger goal. For as long as I could remember, I had wanted to be a headlining magician and mind reader on cruise ships. I hadn't the first clue on how to go about achieving that goal. In fact, living in Ohio, I had never sailed on, or even seen a cruise ship before, but I set the goal anyway.

The Ships

I made up a new set of notecards with the aim of landing a contract with Norwegian Cruise Lines. Napoleon Hill said that it was imperative to include every single detail about your goal. I chose the exact cruise line, which was a random choice, the exact amount of money that I wanted to make, and the exact month that I would be offered a contract. I had no idea how much a cruise line would pay a magician, so I just guessed at a number. The number was more than double my previous goal of $1000 per week. I had nothing to lose, so I gave it a shot.

For several months, I read my new note cards several times per day. I became so obsessed with reaching this goal, that I eventually memorized all twelve of the cards. Each card was completely filled with writing, tiny writing, so that was a lot to memorize. Anytime I found myself driving to a show, I would recite my cruise ship goals out loud, over and over. If a gig were an hour drive away, I would turn off the radio and shout out my goals, at the top of my lungs, for the entire trip.

I only did this when I was driving alone, of course. I didn't want anyone to think I was crazy. I also took action towards achieving this goal. I mailed videos to cruise ship agents, did follow-up calls, and practiced my act each day.

Back then, sending a video to an agent meant physically mailing a VHS tape. Several agents mailed my video back to me with a note saying that they were not interested, but I kept at it. Eventually, I called an agency and asked if they had received my video. They said that they had, but that they weren't interested in working with me. I was actively persistent and continued to call them. I needed to know why they weren't interested and it was difficult to get a straight answer. Eventually, they caved in and invited me to fly out for a live audition at my own expense. The audition would be in front of an entire audience of cruise ship entertainment directors from every major cruise line.

I did the audition and it went perfectly. Out of about thirty acts that auditioned, five of us were invited to have dinner with all of the entertainment directors the evening after the audition. It was during that dinner that I was offered a three-month contract with... you guessed it, Norwegian Cruise Lines. The money that they offered me was even more than the number that I had written on my goal cards, so technically my goal didn't exactly come true. The craziest part was that my contract would begin in July, which was the exact month that I had written down several months prior. It didn't even hit me until a few weeks later, while I was telling this story to a few friends and showing them my note cards, that absolutely everything had happened exactly as I had designed. You see, they were offering to pay me more than I had wished for, but my newly acquired agent was going to take ten percent of that money. Guess what my weekly payment minus my agent's cut equaled? That's right. The EXACT number that I had written down on my cards!

Because of my cruise ship goal, I've been fortunate enough to travel the world for seventeen years, perform for more than a million people, hone my public speaking skills, experience more than 700 cruises, and work for companies like Royal Caribbean, Disney, Celebrity Cruises,

Holland America, and Princess Cruises. I was able to live out my dream of being a full-time entertainer, because I learned how to turn a dream into an attainable reality.

The tricky part about achieving everything that you want is that you can become complacent. I was having so much fun performing on cruise ships, that I stopped reaching for higher goals. I was living the life of a millionaire. No, I wasn't a millionaire, but I certainly felt like one. I traveled the globe, explored exotic beaches, went scuba diving in the world's most coveted spots, smoked Cuban cigars and drank margaritas on exotic beaches, ate the finest foods, met amazing people from dozens upon dozens of countries, and got paid to do it. I was living a Jimmy Buffett lifestyle and I loved it. For nearly seventeen years, I couldn't think of anything else that I'd rather be doing besides being a headlining entertainer on some of the world's most beautiful stages, and so I put my goal setting on pause.

Eventually, I got married, to a beautiful wife, and had three adorable Chihuahuas at home. At this point the goal-setting bug started biting again. I was finally ready for my next big challenge, and that was to become a world-class author, speaker and coach.

When I am performing on cruise ships, which I still thoroughly enjoy, I only have to perform one night per week. For the other six days of the week, I am basically a passenger with an enormous amount of free time. With all of the downtime that I've had over the past seventeen years, I became obsessed with figuring out why the techniques in "Think & Grow Rich" actually worked. I began studying hypnosis, psychology, Neuro-Linguistic Programming, and anything else that has to do with the powers of the mind. I also read hundreds of self-help, goal-setting and motivational books. What I discovered, were ways to streamline, and enhance the techniques that I had successfully used in the past to reach my goals. What you will learn in the following pages is the best of the best, from all that I have learned, tried, and tested. I'm ready to do something exceptional again! Are you with me?

5 HOW FAST YOU CAN EXPECT RESULTS

Knowing is not enough; we must apply. Willing is not enough; we must do. - Bruce Lee

Not a Magic Pill

I've met dozens of people over the years that have the same knowledge that I do. They've read hundreds, or even thousands, of the same books, studied similar techniques, and have spent great sums of money on coaching and motivational courses and seminars, yet are unsuccessful. How can that be? The reason that they're not successful in achieving their goals is that they don't APPLY the knowledge. Having knowledge without applying it is like having a car with no gas. It'll never get you anywhere.

I wish that I could force you take action on the material in this book, but I cannot. This information will either sit idle inside of your brain, or you will use it to reach your greatest potential. Too many people read book after book, take class after class, and go to seminar after seminar, without ever achieving results. They somehow expect the information to automatically transform their lives without them ever having to lift a finger. Well, if it were that easy, then everyone would be successful.

I challenge you to really give the techniques in this book a try. Dive into it, full throttle, for at least 21 days. Some of the action steps might sound silly, or impractical, but what have you got to lose? I can promise you that nothing in your life will change simply by reading a book. But, if you take action, and commit to actually using these techniques, I know that you will be blown away by what you can accomplish. The good news is that nothing in this book is hard to do. In fact, what you're going to learn are simply a collection of easy actions steps that will take nothing away from you except for a little bit of time. But I promise that it will be time well spent.

Before I decided to write this book, I used to share my success system with anyone who would listen. I felt as though I had discovered a secret that everyone needed to know about. I thought that anyone who knew what I knew would instantly apply the system in their own lives and reach any goal that they desired. I was wrong. Most of them never even gave it a shot, but the few who did, were able to produce the same level of results, or even better, than I had.

One gentleman, a cruise director that I had met on my first ship contract, called me after being out of touch for four years. He said, "I just wanted to call and thank you for changing my life. When we met, several years ago, you shared your success system with me, and even gave me a copy of "Think & Grow Rich." I didn't see a use for it at the time, because I didn't know what I wanted my destiny to be. I was content with where I was, but then everything changed. Two years ago, I discovered who I really wanted to become, and I began applying your lessons to a new business venture. Today, I am more successful in my life and in my business than I ever could have imagined, and I owe it to your system and that damn book."

I recently visited this friend at his gigantic house in Texas. He grabbed me by the arm and said, "I have something you have to see." He took me into his office, and hanging on the wall in a picture frame, was the first page of "Think & Grow Rich." It was the page that I had scribbled a message on that read, "You have more potential than most of the people that I know. I know that this book, when in your hands, will have the power to help you achieve something great." It took him four years before he actually applied the techniques in that book. But, when he did, it changed his life in an awesome way. He now runs a company with 217 employees and has purchased a copy of "Think & Grow Rich" for each one of them.

> If I have seen further, it is by standing on the shoulders of giants. - Isaac Newton

Now you're probably thinking, "So why do I need your book, Chad? Why don't I just read "Think & Grow Rich" and go to the original source? Actually, if you haven't already, I suggest that you do read Napoleon Hill's book. In fact, ALL of his books are incredible and you should read each one. My favorite, next to "Think & Grow Rich," is called, "Outwitting the Devil." It's the follow-up to "Think & Grow Rich," but wasn't published until 2011, long after Hill's passing. It deals with some topics that, at that time, were considered controversial, and his wife didn't want him to publish it, so he didn't. Nonetheless, it's a remarkable book. The reason that you should study this book, as well as all of Hill's is that Hill's books were written in the 1930's. Since that time, some of Hill's techniques have been improved upon and streamlined to produce results more quickly and more effectively. His teachings are certainly the foundation for this book, but we will build upon his methods using modern ideas and techniques that science and psychology have discovered about the subconscious mind since that time.

> Don't wait. The time will never be just right.
> - Napoleon Hill

It's Up to YOU

In order for this system to work for you, you must first know what it is that you want your destiny to be. If you're not motivated to become better than you are right now, this will be a waste of your time. You must have an endgame in mind. You must know exactly the person you wish to become. What is your ultimate goal? Figure out what that is before applying this system. Without a chosen direction, the system will fail.

Make sure that your ultimate goal is something that you truly desire, and that you're passionate about it. If you apply this system to something that you're not passionate about, you will find little success and your motivation will run out of steam. We'll talk more about setting up your goals in the chapter on goal setting, but for now, begin to think of what the ultimate you looks like for you. Start to imagine exactly who you'd like to become. Be sure to include every detail that you can imagine. Define what ultimate success looks like through your own eyes. Don't rely on what society views as success. All that matters is what it is in your mind. How much money do you want to make? What kinds of relationships do you want to have? How do you wish to be seen by the rest of the world? What kind of body do you wish to have? Think about everything that you want to be able to look at in your future and feel grateful for. All of this must be considered when creating your destiny.

Whatever you do, do not procrastinate with applying this system towards achieving your destiny. The time to take action is now. Don't let this book be something that sits on your bookshelf with the intent to use it "someday." We are only given a short amount of time on this earth, and achieving your ultimate destiny will not happen overnight. Take action right away. I know how easy it can be to learn a success system, but never apply it. You might read this and think to yourself, "Sure, it worked for you, but it will never work for me." That is nothing more than an excuse to remain content with mediocrity. Don't be like most of the people on this planet. You are special, and you and I both know that you dream of doing something bigger in your life.

This is your ticket to accomplish anything that you can dream of. Mark Twain wrote what has become one of my favorite quotes. It inspires me so much that I keep a printing of it above my desk where I'm forced to see it daily. He wrote, "Twenty years from now you will be more disappointed by the things that you didn't do than by the ones you did. So throw off the bowlines. Sail away from the safe harbor. Catch the trade winds in your sails. Explore. Dream. Discover." Please don't look back on your life in twenty years, and regret not taking action towards creating your deserved destiny. Do not have a fear of failure. Failure is inevitable, so the sooner you can get the failures out of the way, the soon you'll hit your target.

Creating Habits

There will be challenges along the way. Creating massive change in your life is not going to be easy. There will be an enemy trying to stop you at every turn. Your biggest enemy on this journey will be yourself. You see, your mind's made up of two parts. They are the conscious mind and the subconscious mind. It's simple to make decisions in your conscious mind, but reprogramming your subconscious mind will take effort.

Ultimately, it is our subconscious minds that decide who we are. If your subconscious mind doesn't like the conscious changes you're trying to make in your life, it won't allow them to endure. Our subconscious minds hate change and will try to discourage our personal development. It's not that our subconscious minds don't want us to succeed. It's that they don't want us to take risks. In his wonderful book, "The War of Art," author, Steven Pressfield calls this battle of the minds, "Resistance." Pressfield writes:

> Resistance is experienced as fear; the degree of fear equates to the strength of the Resistance. Therefore the more fear we felt about a specific enterprise, the more certain we can be that that enterprise is important to us and to the growth of our soul. That's why we feel so much Resistance. If it meant nothing to us, there'd be no Resistance.

So how can we get our conscious minds to override our subconscious minds? That's the challenging part. Fortunately, in this system, you're going to learn how to do exactly that. You will learn how to reprogram your subconscious mind to, not only agree with, but also eventually champion your conscious mind towards your chosen destiny. The methods that we will use to accomplish this are integrated throughout the entire success system. They include self-hypnosis, repetition, visualization, and the ability to push through fear. We'll talk much more about how and why those techniques work throughout the book. For now, just know that you will have the ability to reprogram your subconscious mind into becoming the exact person that you wish to be.

Make sure that you choose to become the absolute best version of you that you can imagine. Think about it like this. If you find that this stuff really does work, and I'm certain you will, why would you apply it towards creating a slightly better version of yourself? Why not put all of your cards on the table, and shoot for the stars? Don't be afraid to think big. In fact, I want you to imagine your perfect destiny, and then I want you to make it even greater. I want your goal to be so great, that it scares the heck out of you, and then I'm going to help you achieve it.

In the beginning, you might not see massive results. You might not see any results at all, but that doesn't mean that you should give up. It will take time to get the ball rolling, but once it starts, the results will increase exponentially. Just imagine that the work that you're about to put into this is like a heavy boulder that you need to push up a hill. The problem for most people is that they give up before they ever get the boulder to the top of the peak. They simply stop pushing and the boulder rolls back down the hill, crushing their spirit as it does. You've got to keep on keeping on until you get your boulder over the summit. Once it's over the top, everything's literally downhill from there. When you finally begin to see results, they will continue to come in rapid succession. Just know, and believe, that the results that you desire will come, and they surely will.

6 USING YOUR MIND TO PREDICT THE FUTURE

Thoughts become things. If you see it in your mind,
you will hold it in your hand. – Bob Proctor

How Your Mind Can Mold Your Future

I mentioned earlier that when I talk about predicting the future, I'm not talking about predicting the lottery numbers or anything like that. What I am talking about is your ability to mentally create the future that you desire, and then utilize your subconscious mind and The Law of Attraction to make that future a reality. Just so you know, I'm a very skeptical person who doesn't believe in anything supernatural or paranormal. That being said, the things that begin to happen in your life, as a result of using this system, will often seem to happen as if by magic. Napoleon Hill describes this as being able to connect your desires to what he called Infinite Intelligence.

Some people believe that we are connected in some magical way to all of the power that exists in the universe. They also believe that your subconscious mind is your direct link to that power. They believe that if you learn how to manage your subconscious mind, that you can harness this power and the universe will work in your favor. There is zero scientific evidence to support these claims, and as I said before, I'm quite a skeptic to any claims that lack scientific evidence. That being said, whenever I utilize this system, the world really does seem to somehow bend in my favor. I end up accidentally meeting just the right people who can help me achieve my goals. I make seemingly random decisions that end up being imperative to my planned outcome, and I'm suddenly presented with the perfect solution to an impossible problem in a dream. My phone randomly rings at just the right moment, and all of the stars seem to line up in just the right way to guarantee my success. It's as though this system enables you to have some special connection to the universe, and that connection brings with it an endless abundance of good luck. Whatever it is that makes this system work doesn't really matter. What matters, is that it simply works.

If you've ever read the book, or seen the movie, "The Secret," they talk about this phenomenon in detail. I recommend that you watch the movie if you haven't already. The book is great as well, but the movie is fun to watch and it will get you excited to start manifesting. They put a tremendous amount of work into the production value, and it really is inspiring. That being said, there are a few things that concern me about that movie. In "The Secret" they state that, in order to turn your dreams into reality, all you have to do is ask for what it is that your desire, and the universe will deliver. While that is true at the base level, my experience reveals that it's not quite that simple. Think about it. If all you had to do, in order to make the Law Of Attraction work was simply ask the universe for it, and then it would simply manifest in your life, there'd be no such thing as poverty. I guarantee that those suffering from a lack of food, shelter or water are asking and praying for those things to manifest on a daily basis. Yet, their situation fails to improve. So, instead of viewing "The Secret" as a complete guide to success, I view it as an explanation of one part, albeit an imperative part, of the steps to destiny fulfillment.

The part that "The Secret" leaves out is that hard work and a burning desire to succeed are also necessary to achieve your goals. Knowing what you want, and asking for it, is only the first step. What this first step does, is allow you to focus your mind and all of your energy towards achieving your goals. Then, you must take massive action toward reaching them. Without a willingness to do whatever it takes, you're not likely to succeed. You can't just "want" something into existence. You must first want it, then create a burning desire for its attainment, and then do everything in your power to achieve it. If there is a "Secret" power in the universe, it's not going to help you unless you're willing to help yourself.

I know that I'm going to receive a bit of flack from some of The Law of Attraction experts about my belief that hard work is mandatory in order for it to successfully work, so let me give you some examples. I want you to try and think of five super-successful people who simply sit back and watch their dream life magically manifest itself without hard work and hustle. It's tough, isn't it? Ok, maybe the Kardashian's, but they're an exception to the rule. Look at people like Tim Ferriss, Grant Cardone, Gary Vaynerchuk, Bill Gates, Oprah Winfrey, and Russell Brunson. Do these people just sit on their couches and wait for success to magically appear? Not at all. Each one of them wakes up every morning with a burning desire to succeed and then they hustle their butts off to make it happen. Extraordinary success is not a lazy-person's game. But, if you're following your passion, none of this will ever feel like work. In fact, you will find yourself waking up excited each morning, filled with a newfound energy, because you're so determined to tackle your goals.

The scary thing is that the system will work for anyone who applies it. Why is that scary? There are people who would, and who have, used these techniques with malicious intent. The universe doesn't seem to care whether you're a good person or a bad person. I once heard this described through a gardening analogy. If you have fertile soil, sunshine and water, and you plant a seed, the seed will grow. The universe, which is represented by the soil, while the planting, and water represent the work, doesn't care if the seed is that of a beautiful flower or that of a poisonous hemlock plant. If the system is applied effectively to any goal, it will work. I ask that you make certain to only design a destiny that will not cause harm to others. Choose a destiny that will be favorable for you, your family, and the rest of the world. Deal?

> When your desires are strong enough, you will appear to
> possess superhuman powers to achieve.
> - Napoleon Hill

Why Does This System Work?

Since I'm unable to explain, with evidence-backed science, the workings behind the phenomenon that you're about to experience, I'll do my best to share what my personal experiences and research have shown. I talked before about the whole being greater than the sum of its parts. It seems that by applying a combination of all of the techniques, described within this system, you develop a laser-like focus on all of the things that are needed to achieve your predetermined destiny. It's easy to become focused consciously, but what makes this program different and so powerful, is that it also enables you to purposely focus your subconscious mind as well. As I mentioned before, if the vision that you've created for your future is not also accepted by your subconscious mind, your efforts will be futile.

Studying the martial arts can demonstrate a simple example of reprogramming the subconscious mind. I personally studied Praying Mantis Kung Fu, and Brazilian Jiu-Jitsu for many years. My Jiu-Jitsu instructor would teach a series of complicated techniques and expect me to be able to utilize them when sparring or practice fighting. For the first few hundred attempts, the complex chain of techniques would confuse the heck out of my mind. It simply didn't feel natural, and therefore was useless in actual combat. By repeating the moves over and over again, sometimes for several months, they would begin to feel somewhat natural. At this point, the techniques still existed primarily in my conscious mind. Over time, I would find myself dreaming of the techniques while sleeping. The moment that a new series of moves made their way into my dreams, they became second nature. I no longer had to think about doing them. It was no longer a conscious decision. My subconscious mind had finally accepted the techniques as a part of my being, and the moves became automatic.

A large part of this system will be devoted to persuading, and reprogramming, your subconscious mind to accept your chosen destiny as a permanent part of your being. Scientists have found that our subconscious minds have the ability to process 200,000 times more information than our conscious minds. That's a lot of extra power to have under your command!

In order to achieve the highest level of results from this system, you must begin to see yourself as a leader. Without great leadership skills, it will be impossible to achieve your highest destiny. You are not on this journey alone and will need the help of others to help in the fulfillment of your plan. It doesn't matter if your job doesn't require you to be the "boss" of others. True leadership has nothing to do with being a "boss" or telling others what to do. Great leaders inspire others to share the same vision. That is not to say that you must convince others to dedicate themselves to your personal destiny. Instead, you must find inspiring ways to influence others in a way that is mutually beneficial for all parties involved. Zig Ziglar famously wrote in his book, "Secrets of Closing the Sale," "You can get everything in life you want if you will just help enough other people get what they want." Keep that quote in your mind at all times when acting as a leader. Leadership is not selfishness, but is instead the willingness to inspire. Before you can become a great leader, you must first become a master of yourself. The following chapters will show you how.

> People who are unable to motivate themselves, must be content with mediocrity, no matter how impressive their other talents. - Andrew Carnegie

If It's So Easy Then Why Doesn't EVERYBODY Do It?

If it's possible to achieve the exact destiny that we desire, then why doesn't everybody do it? The majority of the world seems to be content with a life of mediocrity, but why? I believe that there are several factors that contribute to this state of complacency. There's a huge difference between wanting something and taking action on it. In order to take action, one must not only be consciously motivated, but also subconsciously motivated. Those who are lacking the latter will never take full control of their destiny. When speaking of success, in terms of financial gain, T. Harv Eker said, "It all comes down to this: If your subconscious 'financial blueprint' is not 'set' for success, nothing you learn, nothing you know, and nothing you do will make much of a difference."

Sure, people will take action in times of desperation, but that's because the subconscious mind views desperation in terms of survival. For example: If you were completely broke, and about to miss a mortgage payment unless you took action, you wouldn't even hesitate to step out of your comfort zone. You'd simply do whatever needed to be done in order to make that payment.

The problem of inaction comes when we're NOT desperate, but just getting by. If there's no fear for survival, the subconscious mind is happy to sit back and do nothing. In fact, it prefers to do nothing. It does not like change. Change means taking risks and trying something new and scary. This desire to avoid change stems from an outdated evolutionary survival trait. Thousands of years ago, taking any type of risk, literally meant risking your life. Those who survived were the ones who stayed within their comfort zones. However, in modern times, the opposite is true. Those who are willing to either go against their natural, and comfortable, instincts, or step out of their comfort zones, are the ones who succeed the most. The limbic system of our brain, or as many call it, our lizard brain, hasn't evolved with the times. Our lizard brain is responsible for our basic survival. It is what causes us to panic, or go into the fight, flight, or freeze mode, when stepping out of our comfort zones. The problem is that our lizard brains can't tell the difference between a life-threatening situation and an action that will move our lives towards greater success.

Outwitting our lizard brains is not easy, and that's why most people never achieve their full potential in life. In order to overcome our natural instincts, we must reprogram our subconscious minds. T. Harv Eker also said, "If you are willing to do only what's easy, life will be hard. But if you're willing to do what's hard, life will be easy." Sometimes, reprogramming your subconscious mind means doing things that are going to make you feel very uncomfortable. You will feel a ton of anxiety building up about taking certain actions. Most people feel that anxiety and stop. Their lizard brains are telling them, nonsensically, that what they're about to do is dangerous.

Whenever you have that feeling in your mind, and you will, just do it anyway. As actor, Jamie Foxx said on the Tim Ferriss Show podcast, "What's on the other side of fear? Nothing." Most people are never willing to see what's on the other side of fear and therefore remain stuck in the same exact place that they've always been.

In this book, we are going to work together, to reprogram your subconscious mind so that you will feel less resistance when taking massive action. In the meantime, whenever you are overwhelmed with anxiety, I ask you to remind yourself of the title of Susan Jeffers' inspirational book, "Feel the Fear and Do It Anyway." If you make this your mantra, I promise that the number of doors that will begin to open for you will amaze you. And these are doors that lead exactly where you desire to go.

Another reason that most people don't, and won't, apply the principles in this book is because of peer pressure. I'm sure that your friends and family want you to succeed. What they don't want, even if it's only at an unconscious level, is for you to surpass their level of success. People are naturally competitive. As soon as you tell them that you're actually taking action towards achieving your ultimate destiny, you will be met with criticism. You'll probably hear things like, "Why would you want to do that?" or "Why can't you just be happy with what you already have?" or "That stuff doesn't work." For many, that's enough to make them quit. Don't let other people slow you down. If they haven't achieved the level of success that you're aiming for, then their advice in this area is meaningless. Just accept that this will happen, and don't hold it against the people who preach it. It's not that they don't care about your wellbeing. They are simply acting out of an unconscious fear of being left behind.

You will encounter several adversaries along your journey, and your friends and family will most likely be some of them. Just know that your biggest adversary will be yourself. Once you're able to conquer yourself, everyone else will become easy. By implementing the system in this book, you will be able to grow into a more powerful and influential person than you could have ever imagined. As you progress through this system, you will be able to apply your newly developed leadership skills to help those around you to rise up to your level. If you can push through their criticism, one day, they will thank you.

7 THE EFFECTIVE WAY TO SET GOALS

A goal set properly is halfway reached. - Zig Ziglar

Write It Down

It's finally time to dive into the methods. Are you ready? The first thing you need to do is properly set your goals. In order to achieve your ultimate destiny, you must first know exactly what it is that you want. You need to set an ultimate goal and put it in writing.

Do not confuse your dreams with your goals. Everyone has dreams, and most of them do not come true. Life dreams, not the sleeping kind of dreams, only exist in your conscious mind. In order to reach your planned destiny, you must transform your dreams into subconsciously accepted goals. Your aim is to decide precisely what you want your life to look like in the future. Dreams are too vague to get your subconscious mind to participate in making them come true. A dream might be that you want to become rich. Well, what the heck does "rich" mean? Ask a hundred people, and you'll get a hundred different answers.

In order for this system to work, you need to write down your goal in extreme detail. The workbook available at the end of the book is designed to make this process easier. If you don't want to write in the book, you can download the workbook by visiting our website at **www.LeadershipMindPower.com/Workbook**. I promise you, that if you skip this step, the system will fail. Putting your goals in writing is a vital measure towards achieving them. Writing down your goals will be the backbone of everything else that is to come in this system. Skip this step, and like a body with no spine, your dreams will collapse.

Before you fill out the goal section of the workbook, I want you to take some time to really decide what it is that you want. Know that, if you apply this system, you are bound to achieve your goal. When choosing your destiny, do not settle for less than becoming the quintessential you. The goal, or destiny, that you choose at this very moment, will shape the rest of your life. Be absolutely certain that the life you choose is the one that you truly desire.

When choosing your destiny, I want you to write down several options. Then, weigh the different options over the course of several days. You might be surprised at how often you'll change your mind as to which version you truly want. Your life's destiny isn't something to be taken lightly. Before moving on with this program, I want you to decide on a destiny that you are absolutely certain you wish to achieve. Do not choose something that you merely "think" you want. Choose the one that you know, with every fiber of your being, that you truly want. Choose one that gives you chills when you imagine it. It is possible to adjust your goals along the way, but it will save you a great deal of time if you decide on the one that you feel the most passionate about from the start. When deciding which path to choose, it is helpful to ask yourself why. Why do you want a particular goal to become your destiny? Then ask why again and again until you are left with one true answer.

For example: You might have a goal of having one million dollars in assets. Then you must ask yourself WHY is it that you want that specific amount. What would that money mean to you and your family? What will you use it for? If the answer is freedom, ask yourself why you want freedom. If you continue to ask yourself why, you will eventually discover the true passion that you can use to drive yourself into action. Money for the sake of money won't do that. Money is arbitrary and will not work as a motivator alone.

Once you've decided on your goal, get specific. This program will not work for generalizations. If your goal is a financial one, do not simply write down that you want to be rich. You must write down the exact amount that you wish to attain. Your subconscious mind does not understand what being rich means, and therefore, it will not work to achieve it. It WILL understand exact dollar amounts, and this is what you must write down if money is your chosen destiny. Instead of choosing money as your endgame, you might want to think bigger than that. Choose something, an ultimate career goal perhaps, that will inevitably lead to the money that you desire. An example, for a real estate investor, might be to own fifty rental properties that produce a specific monthly stream of income. Here, the goal is the attainment of fifty properties. The income stream will come automatically if the right kinds of properties are purchased.

> Don't set your goals too low. If you don't need much, you
> won't become much. - Jim Rohn

> Set a goal to achieve something that is so big, so
> exhilarating that it excites you and scares you at the same
> time – Bob Proctor

Think Big, and Then Think Bigger

When choosing your destiny, I want you to think big. Think VERY big. Imagine that you can become the perfect person that you can possibly envision. Then, go several steps further. How can you make this vision ever better? You want to set your sights beyond what you think is conceivable. Why? It will keep you from creating an imaginary glass ceiling.

You've probably heard of the experiment where fleas are placed into a jar with a piece of glass covering the top. At first, the fleas jump and bump into the glass ceiling. Eventually, the fleas begin to jump just below the glass to avoid hitting it. When the glass ceiling is removed, the fleas continue to jump just under where the glass had been. This is a great metaphor for how high you should set your goals. Aim for the stars and you just might hit the moon.

Another way to look at this is through martial arts. When learning to break a board with a punch or a kick, the martial artist it taught to aim through the board. If they focus on the board itself, they will fail to break it. As Bruce Lee said, "A goal is not always meant to be reached. It often serves simply as something to aim at." Aim for perfection, and settle for greatness. Your goal should be something that is believably obtainable, but big enough that when you reach it, you'll know that the system worked. You'll know that you've accomplished something great.

The next step in the goal setting process is to create a deadline. Write down the exact date that you will achieve your goal. You'll want the amount of time that you give yourself to be slightly less than what feels reasonable. If the length of time is too short, then you will have a difficult time accepting it as plausible. If the allotted amount of time is too long, it will be too easy for procrastination to show its ugly head. When choosing a deadline for your goal, I want you to imagine that it's do or die. Imagine, that success is the only option and that failure will have terrifying consequences. In reality, the only consequence will be that you'll remain where you already are. For some, that's not enough to push them into action. It's more effective to create an imaginary consequence for not achieving the goal. When you're under pressure to take action, you're more likely to do so. I personally use the fear of regret to motivate myself into action. The thought of looking back on today, twenty years from now, and feeling like I didn't do enough, always gets me moving.

Once you've chosen your ultimate destiny, or your ultimate goal, you'll want to create mini-goals along the way. Write down the milestones that will be needed to achieve in order to reach your final desired destination. Think of this like planning a road trip across the United States. If your journey begins in Pennsylvania and your final destination is California, you need to have stops along the way. You'll never reach California without first driving through several other states. Those other states are your stepping-stones along the way. They are required, and cannot be skipped, as you'll certainly need to stop for food and fuel.

Let's say that your destiny is to become a business owner. In order to do that, you must first complete dozens of mini-goals along the way. You'll have to set up the business, design a brand, create a marketing plan, create a website, etc., etc., etc. List as many of the needed steps that you can think of. Along the way, you will probably need to adjust your map, but that's to be expected. We'll talk about being flexible with your plan next. As long as you know where you're going, you will find a way to make it happen. Especially if your subconscious mind is on your side, and because of the system you're about to employ, it will be.

While applying this system to achieving your ultimate destiny, you will inevitably be met with resistance. There are many roadblocks that will likely appear in your path, and so you must be willing to be flexible. If things don't go as planned, or if you have trouble reaching one of your mini-goals, you must find a way to go around them. Because your subconscious mind will be working with you, finding these workarounds will be easier. They will appear to you in the most unlikely ways, but you WILL find your answers. When met with resistance, do not panic. Just know that you will be able to solve any and all setbacks because of your focus. Flexibility is power. Think of the ancient Chinese proverb that says, "A tree that does not bend with the wind will break." Be willing to adapt and adjust your plan as needed. Be flexible and you will not break.

Take Action

The next thing to write down in your goal setting workbook, which can be downloaded at **www.LeadershipMindPower.com/Workbook**, is a solid commitment to taking action. Decide, and write down, all that's necessary, and all that you are willing to do in order to reach your goals.

What sacrifices are you willing to make? How much time are you willing to devote each day to achieving each goal? What do you risk losing, or missing out on, if you don't do these things? Write down all of the action-steps, no matter how small, that you will need to complete. The more you're willing to do, the faster you will reach your goal. Write these down now, as they will be needed later in the chapter on self-hypnosis.

Writing down your ultimate goal, mini-goals, and action-steps that you're willing to take is only the first, but vital, measure towards actually achieving them. Many people put their goals on paper, only to end up filing them away in a drawer of forgotten dreams. In order to actually turn all of this into reality, you must convince your subconscious mind to accept this goal as your reality. You must also sharpen your leadership skills, as they will be needed along the way.

The time to get started with this is now. Take a break from reading, and fill out the goal setting part of the worksheet. If you happen to change your goal before finishing the book, that's ok as you can make changes as you go along. You might find that, as you read this book, your ultimate destiny will expand into territories that you once would not have fathomed. If that happens, that's great. Now is the time to dream about who you truly want to become. Once it's time to put all of the lessons in action, you will want to have decided on a definite endgame.

In the chapter on taking action, we devise a daily action-plan where your ultimate destiny will be secured, and accepted, by your subconscious mind. We will do this using visualization, suggestion, and self-hypnosis. All of these will be explained in great detail in the coming chapters, but first, we must tackle the art of leadership.

8 THE ART OF LISTENING & LEADERSHIP

The ear of the leader must ring with the voices of the people. - Woodrow Wilson

Your Destiny Is Linked Directly To Your Leadership

Without excellent leadership skills, the journey towards your ultimate destiny will be a long and improbable one. Trying to achieve greatness alone is an inefficient, and fruitless strategy. There will be times when you must rely on the help of others in order to make things happen. With great leadership skills, influencing, and persuading others to support your cause, will become easy. The key is to use your leadership skills to inspire others and not to dictate them. You must find a way to guide them towards achieving their own wants before they will be willing to support your mission.

The most effective leadership skill that you must master is the art of listening. Most people are terrible listeners. Instead of listening, they simply wait for their turn to talk. Without truly listening, it is impossible to obtain a deep understanding of another's desires and needs. Often, when we should be listening, we're actually taking part in several conversations in our own minds. We're simultaneously listening to what someone is saying, analyzing their words, thinking about how their words relate to us, and planning what to say next. That is not an effective method of listening, and it's usually obvious to the speaker that we're not completely focused on them and what they're sharing. Instead of using this multitasking method of communication, try breaking it into phases. Science has proven that multitasking in an ineffective approach and it is best to focus on one task at a time. First, only listen to what they are saying, and allow them to finish. Then take a moment to quietly think their message through. Then, repeat it back to them in your own words to show them that you're actually paying attention. Only then should you respond with your own input. You will find, that by listening in this way, people will love communicating with you. It will take practice at first because we're so used to jumping into the middle of someone else's thoughts.

I began to apply this technique, when I first discovered it, while having lunch with someone who I had only known for a short period of time. We'll call him Tom. For an entire hour, I conversed with Tom with a conscious effort to listen completely. Tom loved to hear his own voice, so I hardly spoke a word for the entire hour. Days later, I was talking to a friend of Tom's. Tom had told our mutual friend that he and I had a wonderful conversation and that he really enjoyed talking with me. From my perspective, it wasn't much of a conversation at all. Tom simply talked, and I listened. The point that I'm trying to make is that, when you truly listen to someone, it will make him or her feel appreciated. If they feel that you sincerely care about what they have to say, they will be much more likely to be there for you when you need them.

This method, of thoroughly listening to someone, is especially effective in sales. And let's face it… we're all in sales. Even if you're not selling a product or service, you're still in sales. You are constantly selling ideas, yourself, and your plan to achieve your destiny. In order to be successful in any form of sales, you must be able to give people what they want. The only way to really know what someone wants is to listen. One of my favorite authors, the late Stephen Covey, said it perfectly with the fifth habit from his inspirational book "The 7 Habits of Highly Effective People." The Fifth Habit is "Seek First to Understand, Then to Be Understood." It sounds so simple, but it actually requires a bit of practice. An easy, and covert way of doing this is to ask your significant other, or a friend, to listen in while you talk to others. It's much easier for someone outside of the conversation to notice whether or not you're able to allow someone to finish speaking completely before speaking yourself. With a little practice, you'll become an expert listener whom people love to talk to. Eventually, you'll begin to notice when others are not listening well, and you'll wonder if you ever sounded as uninterested or as rude as they sound. You may even be tempted to buy those people a copy of this book. Wink, wink.

Why We Suck At Listening

So why is it that true listening is so hard for so many people? I think that many people confuse "hearing" for "listening." Just because we hear someone does not mean that we understand him or her. We can hear when someone speaks to us in a language that we've never learned, but we cannot actually listen. At least, not in a manner that can further aid us towards helping them to achieve their goals. Some people feel that, by allowing others to do the talking they're giving up power. It becomes a competition of egos. What they don't realize is that the one who listens is the one with the most power. They are the ones who have the most information, and information, when properly applied, IS power.

Throughout your journey toward achieving your destiny, you will find pieces of the puzzle that will be necessary to create your complete picture, in a plethora of places. Some of those places will be in the words that you hear from others. If you don't master the skill of listening, you're likely to miss out on some of those opportunities. You might still reach your destination without listening, but that is a lonely path and it will certainly take much longer. You must learn to become a sponge. The information that you will require to reach your goals can, and will, come from everywhere. Be open to it, and when it appears, absorb it and then put it to work in your plan.

9 POWERFUL WORDS & HOW TO USE THEM

The difference between the *almost right* word and the *right* word is really a large matter. Tis the difference between the lightning bug and the lightning. - Mark Twain

Powerful Words

As important as listening is, it is equally important to become a great communicator. Listening is only half of an effective communication process. The other half is being able to share your thoughts clearly in a way that will encourage others to listen and respond to you. Because you've practiced being a great listener, the recipients of your words will be more likely to return the favor. Throughout this chapter, we'll be using the term "Speaking," but these skills will also be transferable to writing emails, texts, letters, sales copy, etc. In The Law of Attraction world, it has been said that you become what you think about most. I'll take that a step further by adding that you become what you think about, speak about, and inspire most.

Effective communication can be a delicate tool. Much of how we are perceived by others comes from the words that we use. There are words that I like to call "Powerful Words." Certain words, and the use of those words, can elicit specific emotional responses in our listeners. If you choose the right words, you get the right response. Choose the wrong words, and get an unwanted or negative response.

The tricky part is that everyone on the planet has different personal associations with words, so we're going to focus on words that are, for the most part, universal in their elicited emotional responses. The meanings of words can also be interpreted differently, depending on the tone of voice that they're delivered in. For our purpose, which is to inspire others, the tone should be a friendly, pleasant one. When speaking to others whom you wish to inspire, speak to them as though you were chatting with your best friend. This will unconsciously make them feel a sense of trust and respect throughout the conversation.

It is also important to learn how to adjust your conversation to the receiver. Different people are different types of listeners. Some like to listen with a focus on audibility while others are visual or kinesthetic listeners. We'll dive deeper into the types of listeners and how to use that to your advantage when communicating in a moment.

First, let's talk about power words. Powerful words are words that leaders use to inspire and not dictate to others. Some examples of words that elicit a positive emotional response, and encourage engagement include:

- Trust
- Respect
- Vision
- Achievement
- Leadership
- Belief
- Community
- Love
- Freedom
- Joy
- Ambition
- Friendship
- Mission
- Beauty
- Peace
- Team
- Passion
- Strength

- Journey

These words should be used to create a sense of common vision amongst your followers. It is pointless to lead others toward your personal goals, if in doing so you are not also helping them to achieve theirs. Doing otherwise is not leadership and will eventually lead to failure of your pursued purpose.

Your aim is to create a funnel of positive action where everyone is succeeding toward reaching his or her personal goals. When structured correctly, the achievement of their goals will have a slingshot-effect on the attainment of your predetermined destiny. Think of it like a bucket that, when completely filled, represents the fruition of your ultimate goal. The bucket is being filled, slowly, by dripping water. For every person whose personal goals will be met by helping you reach yours, you will add another source of water, thus filling the bucket more quickly. However, those who you aren't guiding toward achieving their own personal destiny will represent holes in your bucket. Holes that will leak the water you've worked so hard to obtain, leading to a forever partially filled bucket of mediocrity.

Speaking In The Positive

When seeking to inspire others with powerful words and inspirational communication, it is extremely important to speak in the positive. By that, I mean to speak in terms of "Do" and not in terms of "Do not." Recent studies, in neuroscience, hypnosis, and psychology, have revealed that our subconscious minds are dominant over our conscious minds. The studies revealed that thoughts and decisions are made in our subconscious minds moments before they reach our conscious minds. This information is impactful because it is also known that our subconscious minds do not respond in, or even comprehend the negative.

To put it another way, if you say to someone, "Don't screw this up," the subconscious mind only understands, "Screw this up." The negative word, "Don't" doesn't register and the subconscious mind will inadvertently tell the conscious mind to "Screw this up." A simple example of this is asking someone not to think of a pink dinosaur. What will they certainly think of? You guessed it. They'll automatically think of a pink dinosaur. Since the subconscious mind is ultimately in charge, we'll need to avoid doing that. I do a lot of work in the field of hypnosis, including hypnotherapy, stage hypnosis shows, and seminars. A mistake that many people make when trying to utilize self-hypnosis is to state affirmations in the negative. For example, someone who wishes to lose weight will often say to his or her self "I am not overweight." What they don't realize is that they're actually telling their subconscious mind that they ARE overweight. Again, the subconscious mind doesn't register the word "Not." Instead, they should be stating the affirmation in the positive, which could be "I am thin." It sounds like such a simple thing, but it's vitally important. Affirmations should also be spoken in the present tense. "I AM successful," is more powerful than, "I WILL BE successful."

Before speaking to your followers, or better, your teammates, pause and ask yourself whether you're about to speak in the negative or in the positive. Once you get the hang of it, it will become a habit and your ability to influence will greatly increase. I want to run through a few more examples so that you get the hang of it. A common one amongst leaders is the phrase, "Don't be late." Again, you're basically begging for them to be late by stating this in the negative. A better way, is to make the assumption and give them the benefit of the doubt, by saying, "I'll see you there on-time." Another example that I often hear from parents when speaking to their teenagers is, "Don't crash the car." This one makes me cringe. "Drive safely," is a much better choice!

While demonstrating the power of suggestion and hypnosis during my goal setting presentation, I often use the words "Try," and "Can't" to suggest to the participants' subconscious minds that they are unable to do something. For example, after putting them into a suggestible state, I will tell them to imagine that their feet are stuck to the floor.

Then, I'll say, "Try to move your feet, but find that you can't." This suggestion is so powerful that the participants actually find that their feet are truly stuck to the floor. I'll even give them a financial incentive to try and unstick their feet. I'll drop a $100 bill on the floor, only a few feet away from where they're standing, and say that they can keep the money only if they're able to simply walk over and pick it up. Not once, in my 17-year career has a person been able to do it. The words "Try" and "Can't" are so powerful to our subconscious minds that they are able to literally control our physical actions. The point I'm trying to make is that you should always avoid using those words when speaking to others and especially when speaking to yourself. Tell yourself that you'll "try" to do something, and chances are that you'll fail. Tell yourself that you can't...and it becomes your reality. So, remove these negative words from your day to day vocabulary, unless, of course, you're using them in a hypnotic demonstration.

As you begin to practice speaking in the positive, you'll quickly start to notice that your teammates will begin to respond much better to your words. They'll feel more in rapport with you and they won't even know why. In order to create an even better harmony amongst your team, you will want to share this information with them as well. A team of leaders, who all speak in the positive, will have the capacity to create positive momentum much faster than those who speak in the negative.

When you're leading a group of others toward a common goal, you must think of yourselves as a team. For that reason, you'll want to avoid using the words "I" and "You," and instead focus on "We." Of course, I'm not saying to avoid using those words altogether. Certainly, communication would be impaired without them, but there are times when "We" is the much better choice. "I" and "You" cause a feeling of separation and that's not what you want. You want your group to feel that you're in this together and "We" is a much more powerful word for that purpose. As a leader, do not see yourself as being "above" your team. Instead, see yourself as a coach, whose job it is to uncover the hidden genius in your players, so that everyone can win together...as a team.

Understanding Listening Types

There is not a universal, blanket approach to communication. The way you speak to each member of your team will need to be adjusted according to the type of listener that they are. Different people listen and speak in different ways, and knowing this will help you to communicate with them in the most effective, and influential, way. The listening types that I'm referring to are known in NLP as Sensory Perceptual Strategies. Each person on your team will have a unique way of communicating, and if you know how he or she prefers to communicate, your level of influence will be significantly magnified.

There are three general ways that people are hard-wired to communicate. They are visual, auditory and kinesthetic. While we all use a combination of the three, people tend to favor one over the others just like some people favor their left hand over their right. Once you know the method that an individual favors, you will be able to construct your commutation efforts in the most effective way for that particular person.

Also, when speaking to a group of people, it is best to incorporate a combination of all three strategies so as to impact as many people as possible. Keep in mind, that while individuals will favor a particular strategy, the other strategies might also affect them as well. Some people are visual first, auditory second, and kinesthetic third. Other may be kinesthetic first, visual second, and auditory third. There are generally six possible combinations to a person's sensory perceptual strategy, but the key is to discover their primary, preferred method.

Once you know a person's perceptual strategy, you can adjust your communication efforts to fit accordingly. If a person is auditory, you will want to use words that appeal to the sense of sound. If they're visual, you'll use words that appeal to sight, and for kinesthetic, you'll favor words that appeal to touch. The way to find out is to use the listening skills that we discussed previously. You will listen for keywords that will clue you into the person's sensory perceptual strategy.

Here are the words you should listen for to determine a person's sensory perceptual strategy:

Visual Listeners: Those who prefer to communicate in terms of vision will tend to use phrases like...

- That <u>looks</u> good
- I <u>see</u> what you mean
- Keep an <u>eye</u> on that
- How do you <u>envision</u> this

Auditory: Those who prefer to communicate in terms of auditory will tend to use phrases like...

- That <u>sounds</u> good
- I <u>hear</u> you
- I'll keep my <u>ears</u> open
- That's <u>music</u> to my ears

Kinesthetic: Those who prefer to communicate in terms of kinesthetic will tend to use phrases like...

- That <u>feels</u> right
- I <u>feel</u> good about this
- I can <u>handle</u> it
- That <u>moved</u> me

By being aware of the three primary sensory perceptual types, you'll be surprised at how easy they'll become to recognize. Having this information will enable you to adjust your angle of approach when framing your communication efforts. If you find that a person is visual, use words that are also visual. Describe things in terms of colors, hues, beauty, or shapes.

Think of yourself as the author of a book who's describing a scene in full visual detail. Do the same for auditory and kinesthetic communicators. For auditory, speak in terms of sound, and for kinesthetic, speak in terms of textures, touch and physicality. A practical way to do this is to listen to the types of words that they most commonly use, and then feed those words back to them. They'll begin to love communicating with you, even though they won't know why. This is powerful stuff here, so please give it a try.

10 The motion emotion connection

The most important thing in communication is hearing
what isn't said. - Peter Drucker

Nonverbal Communication

Now that we've covered the art of listening for better leadership
communication, we need to talk about another form of conveyance
known as non-verbal communication. The words that a person speaks
can be manipulated consciously, but the unconscious mind is unable to
lie and fortunately, often leaves physical cues. These clues, which are
popularly know in the game of poker as "tells," can give us a better
understanding of what someone is really thinking and feeling. There is
a strong correlation between our emotions and our physical bodies.
Our emotions have the ability to affect us physically, and likewise, our
physicality can have an effect on our emotions.

These phenomena have been referred to as the motion-emotion
relationship and have been proven in multiple scientific studies. The
importance of being able to communicate non-verbally is tremendous.
In his fascinating book, "What Every BODY is Saying.", retired FBI
agent and master of nonverbal communication, Joe Navarro writes,
"Nonverbal behaviors comprise approximately 60 to 65 percent of all
interpersonal communication..." Sixty-five percent! The good news is
that you don't have to learn how to read a person's body language from
scratch. You've actually been doing it, unconsciously, your entire life,
but there's always room for improvement. We'll cover the basics here,

but I highly recommend that you grab a copy of Navarro's book if you truly wish to master the art.

Easy signs to read are a person's posture. Someone who is happy, excited or positive will tend to present a strong posture. They will stand, or sit up straight. Their breathing will be deep and their chin will be up. A person who is feeling sad, bored or negative will tend to slouch, have shallow breathing and keep their chin down. Of course, these changes in physiology will only be apparent if you're not only listening, but also paying attention visually to the individual. This is why face-to-face communication is so much more powerful than email or texting. It's much more difficult to hide one's true feelings in person.

When making observations of nonverbal communication, it is important not to jump to conclusions. It is possible that a person's posture is not accurately representing the emotions that coincide with his or her words. Sometimes, there are outside influences at play. Poor posture can also be a sign of fatigue, poor health, or any number of other causes. You must become familiar with an individual's general body language in order to be able to notice unusual behaviors or changes. You must also be aware of the context of each independent situation, and be able to make an educated guess as to whether their body language is indicative of their feelings toward your current conversation or if they're being influenced by other factors.

According to Navarro, other signs that are easy to read include squinting the eyes and pursing the lips. You can generally tell if a person likes you or not by watching their eyes when they first see you. If they squint, chances are that they're unconsciously trying to block you out and probably don't think too highly of you, at least, at that moment in time. On the other hand, if they arch their eyebrows when they see you, it most likely means that they're genuinely happy to see you. If you notice someone pressing their lips together at a certain time during your conversation with them, it probably means that they're uncomfortable with something you have just said. Learning to watch out for these will take practice, but will eventually become second nature.

Change Your Body To Change Your Emotions

One of the most interesting, and useful, things to know about the motion-emotion relationship is that it works both ways. Your physiology is influenced by your emotions, but your emotions are also influenced by your physiology. In other words, if you wish to change your emotional state, all you have to do is change your physiology. If you know that a person in a positive state generally tends to have good posture, deep breathing, and their chin up, all you have to do to get yourself out of a negative state is adopt the posture of a positive state.

I know that this sounds strange, but recent studies at Harvard University have proved this to be true. In fact, I recently heard motivational speaker, Tony Robbins talk about it. Robbins said, "Science has proven that emotion is created by motion. Harvard did a study that showed that power postures (Such as standing upright like Superman, with your hands on your hips, body upright, and chin up), within two minutes, your testosterone level will increase by 25%, cortisol levels (Stress hormones) drop 20%, and you're more likely to take a risky action." This is remarkable information because it takes away your excuse to not take action when you simply "Don't feel like it." You can consciously put yourself in a state of positive emotion simply by changing your physical stature.

Go ahead and give it a try. Start by putting yourself into a negative physical state. Sit with your shoulders slouched, chin down, and take shallow breaths for two minutes. How does that make you feel emotionally? It probably makes you feel pretty crappy. Now try the opposite. Stand up in a strong power-posture. Keep your spine straight, chin up, shoulders back and put your hands on your hips like Superman. Now focus on taking deep breaths for two minutes. How do you feel now? Incredible right? And all of this without caffeine! Practice this whenever you feel unmotivated to take action. How you feel, is no longer an excuse for inaction. Change your physicality and change your emotion just like waving a magic wand.

A powerful side effect of consciously changing your physical posture is that you will be seen as a more persuasive leader. Those around you will consciously and subconsciously pick up on your "vibes" and know that you are a person to be taken seriously. Even if you don't completely feel the emotional changes right away, your physical gestures, posture, and overall body language will create the illusion to others that you are in complete control. This is the perfect example of "Fake it until you make it" in useful action. The next time you're speaking or communicating with others, stop and ask yourself, "Is my body congruent with the impression that I'm wishing to portray." If it's not, make adjustments. This also will eventually become a habit and you will always appear as the self-confident leader that you are.

11 VISUALIZATION

Where there is no vision, the people will perish. -
Proverbs 29:18

What Is Visualization

The correct use of visualization will help you as a leader and it will also be of essential importance in reaching your planned destiny. Visualization is the ability to see yourself having already achieved your goals in vivid detail. Why is this important? It's important because visualization has the power to program your subconscious mind into accepting your desired outcome as an existing reality.

Without the approval of your subconscious mind, your conscious efforts will be thwarted and your success will be delayed or even prevented. In the next chapter, we're going to talk about magnifying the power of visualization through, affirmations, self-hypnosis or autosuggestion, and actual hypnosis, but first, let's learn how to visualize in the most effective way.

The secret to effective visualization is taking the desired outcome that you want, and transforming it into an image of fulfilled achievement. In other words, in order for visualization to be effective, you must not think about wanting to achieve your destiny, but must visualize having already achieved it. Our subconscious or unconscious minds don't respond to wants. If you visualize "wanting" to achieve an outcome, your unconscious mind will continue to "want" it as well. "Wanting" something to happen can lead to a state of perpetual setbacks. It's similar to speaking in the negative. Your mind will believe that the goal is to continue "wanting" and therefore will continue to do things to keep you "wanting." If instead, you focus on having already achieved the goal, your mind will accept that as your reality, and do everything it can to fulfill it.

The magic of visualization lies in the fact that your subconscious mind cannot tell the difference from intense visualization and reality. In fact, studies have shown that a person's brain activity is the same whether they're actually doing an activity or simply visualizing doing the activity. This is why professional athletes will visualize game scenarios over and over in their minds before actual competition.

As someone who excels in the art of prestidigitation, I use visualization to practice difficult sleight of hand techniques. Certain skills in the art of magic require extreme dexterity. A single sleight of hand technique might require 10,000 or more repetitions before achieving mastery. I have found that combining physical practice with visualization can significantly shorten the process. I'll practice a technique physically until my hands cramp up and I'm forced to stop. Then, I'll switch to visualization. I usually exercise this visualization part as I'm falling asleep. Surprisingly, when I wake up from sleep, I almost always find that my skills have improved significantly.

It's not only magicians who use the technique of visualization. Professional and Olympic athletes, musicians, inventors, and leaders, all experience similar success with visualization. You may have heard of the study conducted by Australian psychologist, Alan Richardson, who famously tested visualization with basketball players. In the study, Richardson divided basketball players into three groups. The first group practiced shooting free throws for twenty minutes each day. The second group only visualized shooting free throws each day, but never actually touched a ball. The final group did no visualization and no actual shooting. The results of the study showed that the group who only visualized improved their actual shooting only slightly less than the group who practiced shooting physically. The key to making visualization work for you is to make sure you're doing it properly.

Incorporating All Of Your Senses

The proper, and most powerful way, to utilize visualization, is to make the experience as realistic as possible. You must allow your imagination to open wide and make the scenario as vivid as you're able. To do that, you must incorporate all five of your senses. The more vivid and real you can make your visualization, the better. Now, I don't know· what your specific planned destiny is, as it will be different for every reader, so let's just make one up and use it as an example. Let's suppose that your desired destiny is to make five hundred thousand dollars, in a single month, from selling teddy bears online. I'm not sure why that popped into my mind, but let's go with it. How can you incorporate all five senses into that? Let's look at them one at a time.

Visual:

For visual, you might want to imagine yourself sitting down at your computer and logging into your shopping cart account. Don't make this vague. You'll want to see every detail as though it were really happening. What does the room look like? How is the lighting in the room? What are you wearing? Do you see anyone else in the room? What is on your computer screen before you go to your shopping cart? What are the colors that you see? What else do you see on your desk? The more details you can imagine, the more realistic this will become for your subconscious mind. Are you imagining yourself in the office that your currently have, or are you imagining this in an office of the future? All of these things matter. Perhaps you're not even in your office. Maybe you're checking this from your cell phone while having lunch at a cafe, or while sitting on a beach with your laptop. Whatever it is, make it look, and feel, very real.

A great technique, that myself and other people have used with extraordinary success, is to create a vision board. A vision board is a collage of pictures of everything that you desire to attain. There are many ways to create one of these boards, but here's how I've made mine. I purchased a very large cork-board and hung it on the wall in my office where I'm certain to see it often. Tacked to the board are photographs of things that represent my goals. You could have a picture of your ideal house, the car you want to own, an image of the amount of money you wish to acquire, a vacation you dream of taking, the types of relationships you wish to have, etc. By seeing these images on a daily basis, your visualization sessions will become more detailed, vivid and effective.

Audible:

What sounds do you hear in the room? Can you hear the air-conditioning, dogs barking, your children playing? If you're typing on your keyboard, you should imagine hearing the keys being pressed. Perhaps you can hear yourself breathing or hear the sounds of people talking in another room. Is there music in the room? If your personal visualization involves another person, what do they sound like? What is the tone of his or her voice? Does their clothing make noise when they move? At what pace are they speaking to you? Take in all of the sounds in as much detail as you can.

Kinesthetic:

What do you feel? Do you feel they keyboard as you type? How do your clothes feel against your body? What is the temperature in the room? How soft is the chair you're seated in? How do you feel physically and emotionally at the moment of reaching your destiny? Do you feel hungry, full or indifferent? Every piece of information that you can imagine will help to make this more real in your mind. Of course, you don't want to imagine things that you don't actually want to have happen. Keep it positive.

Smell:

What does the room smell like? Is there coffee on your desk? How does it smell? Are you wearing cologne or perfume? If so, are you able to smell it?

Taste:

Unless you're eating, drinking or chewing gum in your visualization, taste probably won't be much of a factor. But, let's say you're the type of person who puts your pencil or pen on your lips when you're working. If you are, you'll want to imagine that taste as well. Again, anything that makes this situation feel real should be included. If your vision involves food, for example, maybe your destiny includes eating at the finest restaurants in the world, imagine what you would order. Imagine how amazing every bite is going to taste, then actually taste it in your mind.

When using visualization, don't be afraid to allow your imagination take over. Visualization should be practiced in a very relaxed state. More on that in the next chapter, but for now, just know that you might have new and useful ideas popping into your mind during this process. If that happens, write them down immediately.

Attaching Emotion & Gratitude

Visualization without emotion is like a Lamborghini without gas. It will get you nowhere fast. In order to ignite and give life to your visualization efforts, you must learn to attach emotion to them. When taking time to visualize the destiny you wish to achieve, which should be several times throughout each day, imagine the exact emotional feelings that would correspond with that achievement. Then, allow yourself to actually feel those emotions. Sure, at first, you might have to fake it as we talked about before. But, fake it until you make it, and eventually you'll begin to feel a real sense of euphoria during your visualization sessions.

In order to fake it until you make it, think about what the physiology of your body would be like if you were actually feeling those emotions. Then, put your body into that physical state. Most likely, you'll want to stand up tall, keep your chin up, breath deeply and smile, laugh, or even cry out joyfully. Whatever you imagine your body doing when feeling the emotions that go along with your achievement, do it. As we mentioned before, the motion-emotion relationship will cause your body to adjust accordingly, and the emotions will eventually become real. This step is vital in the visualization process because without it, your subconscious mind will have trouble accepting your vision as being your reality.

Particular emotions, that you'll want to incorporate, include pride, courage, gratitude, excitement and enthusiasm. You are overjoyed with what you have accomplished. You set a goal, and did everything in your power to achieve it. You made it happen and you deserve to feel proud. You'll also want to feel gratitude while visualizing. Feel grateful for your ability to continue on this path through fruition. Feel thankful for the people in your life who helped you along your journey. Gratitude for the ideas the led you to this point, and gratitude that you had the guts to take all of the action steps that were necessary in transforming your dream into a reality.

Finally, allow yourself to feel excited and happy. You might even want to do a "Happy dance," as though you have just scored the winning touchdown for your favorite football team in the Super Bowl. Now is your time to glow as you feel a rush of energy flowing throughout your entire body. With enough practice, you will actually experience a release of dopamine and adrenaline in your body. You'll feel your heart rate increase, you'll get a burst of energy, and you will be overcome with an incredible sense of well-being. When you feel that, you know you're doing it right and your subconscious mind will have been activated and invigorated.

12 The Secrets of Hypnosis

He who looks outside, dreams; He who looks within,
awakens. - Carl Jung

Direct Paths To The Subconscious Mind

As mentioned throughout this book, in order to achieve your planned destiny, you must be a leader. Leaders are not born, but are forged out of experience, determination and focus. Those of us who are in positions of leadership, which is all of us, in some form or another, should strive to reach our highest leadership potential. If you're struggling to become the leader and achiever that you aspire to be, then, the solution may be found in a lack of congruence between your conscious and subconscious minds.

In order to be a great leader, you must have a leadership mentality. A leadership mentality exists in two parts: external (conscious) leadership and internal (subconscious) leadership. If you wish to reach your full potential, you'll need to master both. But how do we do that?

Having a destiny achieving and leadership mentality isn't something that you do only when you feel like it. It is something that must be formed into a consistent habit and therein lays the problem. Habits are hard to break and equally hard to create. The reason habits, or non-habits, are so rooted in us is because our subconscious minds simply do not like change, and will do everything they can to avoid it. You can consciously tell yourself that you are a great leader and that you have a burning desire to achieve your destiny, but if your subconscious mind doesn't share the belief, it will lead to confusion, doubt, and failure.

Most people give up when trying to change a habit for this very reason. How many people do you know who consciously said that they were going to quit smoking, start exercising, or begin reading more, only to find themselves resorting back to their old ways after a day or two? Their attempt foundered because they failed to get their subconscious minds onboard with the decision. Your subconscious mind doesn't care whether a habit is good or bad for you. It simply wants to go on doing whatever it's become accustomed to doing over time.

The good news is that there are powerful ways to get your conscious and subconscious minds to play nicely together. They are visualization, which we already talked about, autosuggestion through affirmations, and hypnosis. Before I explain each one and how to use them, let's talk about how and why they work.

Your subconscious mind is the one that's always running in the background. It's working whether you're awake or asleep. It fuels your dreams, drives your creativity, ignites your imagination, and most importantly, drives your intuition. It also has final authority over your conscious mind. Whatever takes hold in the subconscious mind is instinctively acted upon by the conscious mind. The subconscious mind is not fickle and has established its preferred ways throughout your entire lifetime. Your conscious mind is your awakened mind that you use for thinking, communication, and physical activities. While the conscious mind can process 40 bits of data per second, the subconscious mind can process 40 million bits per second, and that is why we must tap into its power.

In order to get an idea, thought, or belief from your conscious mind into your subconscious mind, you have to get past the critical factor. Think of the critical factor as a barrier, or gatekeeper, that keeps the subconscious mind from being altered. There are times when the critical factor's guard is down and the subconscious mind becomes more open to suggestions. This can happen quickly, like during a traumatic experience, or slowly if the mind is repeatedly exposed to information over a period of time. Fortunately, there are quicker ways that avoid traumatic experiences, that we can practice to consciously mold our subconscious beliefs to our benefit. In a sense, we can actually reprogram our subconscious minds for success.

Before applying any of the reprogramming methods we're about to cover, you must have a clear vision of what being a great leader means to you, and what you want your destiny to be. The attributes of having a leadership mentality might include:

- Great listening skills
- The ability to inspire others
- A willingness to trust your intuition
- The ability to communicate effectively
- A willingness to expand your comfort zone
- The ability to rule your emotions
- Persistence
- Etc.

As for your destiny, re-visit what you've written down in the goal setting section of the workbook.

Once you've defined what being a great leader and fulfilling your destiny means to you, you can begin to upload them into your subconscious mind through autosuggestion, affirmations, and hypnosis.

Autosuggestion & Affirmations

Autosuggestion is the practice of placing ideas into your subconscious mind through repetition. The more frequently a concept is focused upon consciously, the faster it will be accepted subconsciously. Napoleon Hill described it like this, "Any idea, plan, or purpose may be laced in the mind through repetition of thought." He added, "Your ability to use the principle of autosuggestion will depend, very largely, upon your capacity to concentrate upon a given desire until that desire becomes a burning obsession." We become what we think about most, so think mostly about what you WANT to become.

In order to guide your thoughts toward becoming the leader and achiever, that you desire to become, surround yourself with a sensory overload of those thoughts. The more exposure you have, the easier it will be for them to be absorbed and adopted by your subconscious mind. There are endless ways to do this, and you'll want to incorporate ways that touch as many of your five senses as possible.

Examples of this include:

Note Cards:

Write your affirmations on note cards and read them out loud, or even quietly if in public, to yourself several times a day. The most important times to read them are first thing in the morning, and just before sleep. What you focus on as your drift off to dream will have an easier path into your subconscious mind, as your critical factor will be more relaxed during that time.

Sticky Notes:

Write your most important leadership and goal achieving affirmations, in the present tense, on sticky notes, or on anything else, and distribute them in places that you're certain to see them throughout the day. Your bathroom mirror, your computer desktop image, and on your treadmill in line with your eyes, are a few examples to get you started.

Custom Audio Recordings:

You can also create audio recordings, where you record your affirmations mixed with your favorite music to listen to while you exercise or while driving to and from work. You can also create these without music, but I prefer to do it with. Before you know it, you'll actually feel your mindset beginning to change and these words will become a part of the fabric of your being.

While repetition is great, the effect is greatly amplified if you're able to attach emotion to the stimuli. Don't just read the words. Listen to the recordings, and look at the pictures that you compiled when creating your vision board. Whenever possible, try to imagine yourself having already achieved your leadership and destiny goals and use your imagination to feel the emotions that will go along with those achievements. Einstein said, "Imagination rules the world," and he was right.

One of my favorite techniques to use with affirmations is to choose one and recite it, out loud, throughout the course of a long drive. For example, I might recite the phrase, "I have an abundance of wealth," over and over again while driving for an entire hour. To keep it from getting too monotonous, I'll mix up the sentence each time by emphasizing a different word each time I say it. First, I'll emphasize the word "I," then the next time emphasize "Have," then "Abundance," etc., etc. I know this sounds like a strange thing to do, and I wouldn't do it if I had a passenger in the car, but it works marvelously! Sometimes, I'll do this without the radio on, but other times I'll make a game out of it, and try to say the affirmation to whatever song comes on the radio. After doing this for an entire hour, you'll actually begin to FEEL the phrase sinking into your subconscious. Give it a try and you'll see what I mean.

Proactive Daydreaming:

Most people tend to slip into a trancelike state about one thousand times per day. We call it daydreaming, but daydreaming is actually a trance-like state that is very similar to the state of hypnosis. We usually allow our daydreaming to happen organically. We simply allow our minds to go wherever they choose to go without so much as a conscious thought about it. When you are daydreaming, it is your subconscious mind that is active and not your conscious. This means that the information that we're focused on while daydreaming will have direct access to our subconscious mind. When you begin to truly focus your attention on your goals through autosuggestion and affirmations, you will start to be able to control your daydreams. I call this proactive, focused, or productive daydreaming. The next time you "space out," try to focus your mind on your goals. Just imagine the power of reinforcing your planned destiny, into the most powerful part of your mind, a thousand times per day!

Hypnosis:

If you're serious about getting your subconscious and conscious minds to be congruent, hypnosis is the fastest approach. Hypnosis, especially when combined with auto suggestion through affirmations, and visualization, is exceptionally powerful at creating laser-like focus in both your conscious and subconscious minds.

I was personally a skeptic when it came to hypnosis for many years. While performing on cruise ships, I was exposed to some of the best stage hypnotists in the world. I would watch as volunteers from the audience would come on stage and act out in ridiculous scenarios. These were scenarios that were completely out of character for many of these people. Their personalities would be altered, they would see things that were not there, and they would remember things that never happened. I saw people instantly overcome fears and phobias, and even believe that they were different people altogether, sometimes even believing that they spoke an entirely non-existent language, like Martian.

At first, I had simply assumed that the audience members were just "playing along" with the hypnotist. After seeing this phenomena time and again, I began to take a closer look. I started to read scientific books and journals about hypnosis. I studied the work on hypnosis conducted by brilliant minds such as Sigmund Freud, Milton Erickson, and Dave Elman, and eventually traveled to personally train with one of the best stage hypnotists that I had seen. What I discovered blew my mind. It wasn't hype. This stuff was for real.

If you've tried hypnosis before, then you can already attest to its effectiveness. Others may be skeptical of hypnosis so far as to claim that it's nothing more than imagination at work, but recent scientific studies prove otherwise. The Stanford University of Medicine conducted one such study. In the study, Dr. David Spiegel, who is one of America's leading psychiatrists, used brain-scanning technology to show that different areas of the brain "light up" when a person is under hypnosis. The areas that "light up" in a hypnotized individual are different from a person who is simply using their imagination. The study revealed that, when people are in a hypnotic state, their brains accept the hypnotist's suggestions as reality. In an example from the study, if subjects were told, under hypnosis, that they were seeing a color, their brain would experience seeing that color in the exact same way that they would see it in reality. Spiegel said, "This is scientific evidence that something happens in the brain when people are hypnotized that doesn't happen ordinarily."

In an article in The New York Times, author Jane E. Brody writes this about hypnosis:

> In effect, hypnosis is the epitome of mind-body medicine. It can enable the mind to tell the body how to react, and modify the messages that the body sends to the mind. It has been used to counter the nausea of pregnancy and chemotherapy; dental and test-taking

anxiety; pain associated with surgery, root canal treatment and childbirth; fear of flying and public speaking; compulsive hair-pulling; and intractable hiccups, among many other troublesome health problems.

If we know that hypnosis works, and I sincerely believe that it does, how then can we apply it towards becoming better leaders, and reaching our planned destinies? The answer is to use hypnosis to reprogram our subconscious minds into accepting our future self as already being our current reality. When we do this, The Law of Attraction can go to work in our lives at full-throttle.

Puzzle Pieces

Hypnosis, from my experience, especially when combined with auto suggestion through affirmations, is the most effective way to align your conscious and subconscious minds, and you may find yourself tempted to rely on it alone, but do not. You will see much faster results toward achieving your planned destiny if you accept that it is only one piece of the needed puzzle. Yes, it's a big piece, but not the only piece, and we want to produce the complete picture.

To show you what I mean as hypnosis being only one piece of the needed puzzle, I want you to think of yourself as piece of steel, and in order to achieve your ultimate destiny, you will need to magnetize that yourself so that you will become strongly attracted to your desired destiny. Just so you know, I'm only using steel and magnetism as a metaphor. I'm not suggesting that we are "actually" magnetically attracted to our goals. Instead, this reference is to show you how focusing your mind, in as many ways as possible, toward the achievement of your goals, will help you succeed more quickly.

Imagine that everyone on earth is represented by a hunk of steel. Most of these people are not magnetized. In most people's lives, they are unfocused and haphazardly surviving life by reacting to whatever comes their way. They might be hoping, praying, or wishing to fulfill a destiny, but they are not focused. An unfocused, or demagnetized person would look like fig 1 with the arrows representing focus & the target representing their goals:

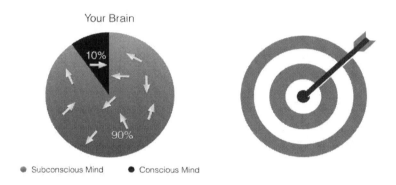

Your Brain

Subconscious Mind   Conscious Mind

fig 1

Sure, their conscious minds might be focused on their goal, but their subconscious focus is scattered. In order to magnetize steel, as many of the polarities, represented by the arrows, as possible need to be in alignment. The magnet will be stronger by having more of the polarities facing in the same direction. Our goal with combining visualization, affirmations, and hypnosis, is to align our focus in as many areas, and in as many ways, as is possible. The more we saturate our subconscious minds with what we consciously want, the more arrows we're able to align. We want our polarities to look more like (Fig 2) so that we're attracted to our goal and our goal is attracted to us likewise.

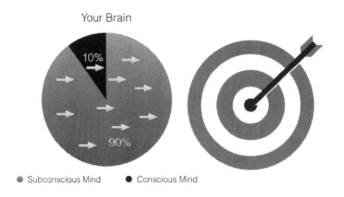

Your Brain

Subconscious Mind   Conscious Mind

fig 2

Using only one of the techniques is like magnetizing the rod by banging it against a pole, which can actually be done. How do I know this? I saw it on an old episode of MacGyver, so it's got to be true. Banging it against a pole can eventually magnetize steel, but we want results more quickly and predictably. When you combine all of the methods described, it's like wrapping that globe in copper wire and sending electricity through it. Now you have a MUCH more powerful electromagnet, or in our case, a much more powerful, and focused, subconscious mind.

Some Hypnosis Facts

One of the great things about using self-hypnosis, besides the fact that it can be extremely effective, is that it doesn't take a long time to implement and it costs very little or no money to get started. All that is needed to experience the power of hypnosis is your commitment to giving it a try and your ability to stick with it until it works. Some people will experience dramatic results was a single hypnosis session while others might require several sessions. I recommend that you use hypnosis at least once per day until you begin to feel the benefits. Once you find that it's working, you can continue to use it as needed.

First, I want to explain what hypnosis actually is and also what it is not. Hypnosis is not some form of mind-control, voodoo or magic. At its heart, hypnosis is simply a way of relaxing your mind in such a way that your subconscious mind is brought to the forefront. When in this meditation-like state, your critical factor will be lowered, and the suggestions that you give yourself will be easily accepted as your reality. Without hypnosis, the same suggestions will likely be met with resistance and will not be adopted as new life habits.

I also want to tackle some of the fears and questions that are often expressed whenever I speak about hypnosis. Many seem to fear that they might get stuck in a trance-like state while under hypnosis. This is something that you don't have to fear at all as it is actually impossible for this to happen. In fact, if I were to hypnotize you right now and then decide to leave you alone, after a minute or two of not hearing my voice, you would simply wake up and be back to full conscious awareness. While you're under hypnosis, it will not actually feel like anything other than relaxation. During a normal day, most of us slip in and out of hypnosis several times. If you've ever been driving somewhere, that you've driven to many times before, and you suddenly realize that you've completely missed your exit, you were experiencing what is known as highway hypnosis. What happens here is that your conscious mind is busy thinking about something else, so your subconscious mind takes over driving the car. It does this to keep you safe, as that's one of its most important jobs. The problem is that, while your subconscious mind knows how to drive the car, it does not know where you wish to go, so it just keeps on driving.

Being hypnotized is not difficult to do and will not require too much effort on your part. All that you have to do is follow the steps that we'll discuss shortly, and then just allow yourself to relax. As long as you focus your mind on the suggestions that you're hearing and allow your imagination and subconscious mind to go to work, you will easily become hypnotized. I've been asked often if it's easier to hypnotize someone who is not intelligent or who is weak-willed, and the answer is no. Actually, the opposite is true. It has been scientifically proven, that in order to be a good hypnotic subject, you must have an average or above average level of intelligence. This is because it is easier for an intelligent person to focus his or her thoughts for an extended period of time. The more you're able to relax your body and mind, and the more you're able to focus your attention on the suggestions that you will be hearing, the more effective your sessions will be.

During your self-hypnosis sessions, you will not actually be asleep. Even though hypnotists often use the word sleep, the state of hypnosis is not the same thing. Under hypnosis, you are fully conscious, awake, and aware of what's going on around you. Sure, some people become so relaxed that they actually do fall asleep, but that's not the case for most. If you're afraid of falling asleep during your sessions, you might want to set an alarm just so you're not late for an appointment. Finally, in order to be hypnotized, you must actually want it to work. If you are too apprehensive and don't actually try to relax and follow the suggestions, then you will not be hypnotized. For some, it might take a bit of practice before you can allow your mind to truly relax. Sometimes, there might be too much on your mind for you to focus your attention long enough to reach a trance-like state. Just know that anyone can become hypnotized under the right conditions, so if it doesn't work the first time, don't give up. It may just mean that you were too preoccupied with other things at the time.

For the sake of this book, you will want to use your self-hypnosis routine to help you in the achievement of your destiny, but its use is not limited to only that. Once you understand how to hypnotize yourself, you will be able to create audio sessions that can help you lose weight, quit smoking, exercise more, alleviate aches and pains, ease stress, help you sleep, and more. In fact, you can apply self-hypnosis to any area of your life. Of course if you're dealing with a medical or psychological condition, it is best to seek the advice of your doctor first. While hypnosis is very powerful, and has the ability to cure all types of problems, it should never be used as a replacement for professional medical attention.

Creating Your Personal Self Hypnosis Sessions

I'm going to walk you through an example of how you can create your own self-hypnosis sessions. The easiest way to do this, and the method that I personally use, is to create an audio recording of your session. Basically, you will be writing out a hypnosis script that you will then read out loud and record. You can then mix your recording with relaxing background music. I recommend downloading hypnosis music, meditation music, or what are known as binaural beats to play quietly in the background. You can record your voice using the voice recorder on your smart phone, or by using audio recording software on your computer. Audacity is a great one that is free to use. If you need help figuring out how to mix music with a voice track, there are many tutorials available on YouTube that will show you how. It's quite easy, so if you're not computer savvy, don't fret.

Your self-hypnosis session and script will be broken down into five parts.

1.Create Your Mindset
2.The Hypnotic Induction
3.Deepening the Trance
4.Your Personal Suggestions
5.Awaken Back to Full Consciousness

Create Your Mindset

Creating the right mindset before your self-hypnosis session will make it easier for the suggestions to work. You will want to make sure that you are in a location where you will not be disturbed for the length of your session, which is generally about 3--minutes. Find a relaxing, quiet space where you can either sit comfortably or lie down in a comfortable position. If seated, you will want to have both feet flat on the floor and your hands in your lap. Keep your hands separate from one another so that they are not touching. While getting ready to listen to your recording, take a moment and focus on your "Why." What is it that you wish to accomplish with today's session? What changes do you wish to create in your subconscious mind and what will these changes bring to your life?

The Hypnotic Induction

The purpose of the induction is to completely relax your body and your mind. This will allow your subconscious mind to become open to the suggestions that it is about to be given. The induction process will help to lower the critical factor and shift your mind from the external to the internal. When the critical factor is bypassed, your subconscious mind will become receptive to the changes that you wish to make in your life. Once these changes are accepted by your subconscious, they will become your new habits and will no longer be fought by a resistance to change.

Deepening the Trance

There are several levels of hypnosis, and in order to achieve the best results, you want to go as deep as possible. The deepening stage of the induction is designed to do just that. You will be listening to a countdown that will relax your body and mind even more. This part of the induction is what separates hypnosis from mere relaxation. The deepening will put your subconscious mind into a state of complete and unjudged acceptance.

Your Personal Suggestions

Once your subconscious mind is relaxed and open to accepting new ideas and information, you will begin to hear your suggestions. These suggestions should be aligned with your goals and include the changes that you wish to make in your life. For each hypnotic session that you create, you will only want to focus on one or two primary suggestions. In other words, don't have a single self-hypnosis session include every single goal that you wish to achieve. Focus on the most important ones, and then create new sessions for your other goals. As mentioned earlier in the book, it is vital that your suggestions are spoken in the positive. Remember that the subconscious mind does not comprehend phrases spoken in the negative. For example, if you were making a suggestion about stage fright, you would NOT want to say, "I am not afraid to speak in public." That sentence would be understood by your subconscious as meaning that you ARE afraid to speak in public because it would omit the word "not." Writing out your suggestions will be very easy. All you have to do is go back to your daily affirmations and use those as your suggestions. And, since those have already been written in the positive, they should be good to go as is.

Awaken Back to Full Consciousness

After the relaxation and suggestions, you will include an awakening section on your recording. In this section, you will count yourself up, and back to full awareness, from one to five. With each number, you will be solidifying the suggestions and reaffirming that they have been accepted by your subconscious mind. The awakening sections will also leave you feeling wide-awake and full of energy. Skipping this section might leave you feeling sleepy and too relaxed to do anything productive for a while. When done correctly, the awakening will fill you with a burst of energy and enthusiasm that you can carry with you for the rest of the day.

Now that you understand the basic format of a self-hypnosis session, I'm going to provide you with a sample script. As most of the people reading this book will have different goals in mind, the suggestions that you use will probably be different from my example. The induction, deepening, and awakening sections can remain identical for all of your self-hypnosis recordings.

A Sample Self-Hypnosis Script

(The Induction) – Record yourself reading this script. Adjust the suggestions to fit your goals. When editing in the relaxing music, let the music play for 20-30 seconds before the speaking begins. The script should be read slowly. Feel free to pause in order to allow yourself to take action on the instructions that you will be giving to yourself. Try to use a relaxing tone and volume when recording as this will help to make listening to this more hypnotic.

Begin Script:

Just begin to take some nice, slow, deep breaths as you begin to relax your body. Breathing in through your nose...and out through your mouth. On the count of three, take a very deep breath. One, two, three, inhale....hold it...and exhale... Good. Let's take another deep breath on the count of three. One, two, three, and inhale...hold it...and exhale slowly... That's it. And now the deepest breath...one, two, three, inhale...and this time, as you exhale, just allow your eyes to close.

Focus only on the sound of my voice, blocking out all other sounds and distractions. From this moment on, with every breath you exhale, and with every sound of my voice, just allow yourself to relax even deeper. Focus your attention on the chair you're seated in, or on the surface you're lying on. Notice how that chair supports your body completely and how you needn't do anything at all...but relax. Now, move your attention to your right arm. Relax that right arm completely, allowing every muscle to just completely switch off. Just releasing all tension and stress from that right arm... That's it....good...

Now perhaps you become aware of your left arm. Notice how that left arm is completely supported by your leg, and just allow every single muscle and fiber in that left arm to completely let go. To completely relax, and allow that feeling to drop your mind down into an even deeper state of relaxation... Just increasing that relaxation with each and every breath that you exhale.

79

Now imagine that relaxation in your arms beginning to rise up from your fingertips all the way into your biceps… into your triceps, and rising up into your shoulders. Every muscle, completely loose, limp and relaxed. Now just allowing that relaxation to float down your chest, and down your back, just letting go of all tension, and as you do, noticing how good and relaxing it feels. Feel that relaxation melting down your lower back and stomach, all the way down into your thighs.

Just feeling as though your entire body is becoming as relaxed and limp as a wet towel. Or imagine that your entire body is made from a handful of loose rubber bands. Once your thighs are completely relaxed, just allow that relaxation to continue into your knees…down into your calf muscles…and then all of the down, washing over your ankles, and into your toes. Every muscle, completely loose, limp, and relaxed.

And as you continue to breath, and listen to the sound of my voice, just allow yourself to drop down into an even deeper state of complete, and total relaxation. Now, just allowing that relaxation to wash all the way from your toes, back up your legs, up your spine, and all the way into your neck. Relaxing those neck muscles completely and just allow your heavy head to gently fall forward into a more comfortable and relaxing position.

Now, just focusing your attention on the muscles in your jaw, and just allowing those muscles to completely switch off. Completely relaxed, feeling so peaceful…so comfortable…so relaxed. And now, just allow that relaxation to rise up into the muscles around your eyes…and the muscles in your forehead. Just letting go of all tension and stress throughout your entire body…and as you do, noticing how good and relaxed you feel. And with each and every sound of my voice, and with each breath that you exhale, just continue to allow yourself to drop down deeper. The deeper you go, the better you feel. And the better you feel, the deeper you go.

If at anytime you need to awaken, I want you to understand that all you have to do is count yourself up from one to five, and you will immediately be completely awake and alert.

Now, I want you to remember a time in your life when you felt completely relaxed and peaceful. A time when you had no stress...no cares and no concerns... And I want you to go back to that time in your mind. See everything that is around you at that peaceful, relaxing time. Smell the smells. Hear the sounds...and just allow this memory to drop yourself into an even deeper state of relaxation.

(Deepening the Trance)

Now that your body is relaxed, we're going to relax your mind. In a moment, I'm going to count backwards from five to one. I want you to imagine yourself standing at the top of a staircase. With each number, imagine yourself moving down the stairs, and with each and every step down, just allowing yourself to drop down even deeper to a point to total and complete relaxation. Each and every time we do this, it will drop you down twice as deep, so that you can feel twice as good, twice as confident, twice as relaxed...your imagination is opening wide...you feel wonderful.

Five...just letting go of all cares and concerns

Four...feeling so completely relaxed in every way

Three...dropping down even further and deeper now

Two...releasing all thoughts from your mind...and

One...dropping all the way down to a place of complete and total serenity

We're going to do this one more time so that you can feel even better. Even more relaxed...even more peaceful...this time dropping you down one hundred times deeper, relaxed...

Five…releasing every care and concern

Four…feeling even more relaxed in every way

Three…dropping down one hundred times further and deeper now

Two…pushing all thoughts from your mind…and

One…dropping all the way down, and as you do, noticing how wonderful you feel…

(Your Personal Suggestions) (In this example, we will use "Self-Confidence" but you will plug in your personal affirmations here. The suggestions portion of the session can be as long, or as short as you like)

From this moment on, I want you to understand that every suggestion that I give you will be completely accepted by your subconscious mind. Each and every suggestion will become your reality. When you have accepted this…just simply nod your head…that's it…good.

I want you to understand something special about yourself. I want you to understand that you have complete self-confidence…

You know that you have the power, the ability, and the capacity to do anything that you put your mind to…

You have complete self-confidence…

You take immediate action toward your goals and you achieve your goals.

You take action every single day to turn your goals into your reality.

You are a powerful person with gifts that no one else has.

You have the ability to achieve any goal that you desire…

You have complete self-confidence...every day...in every way...

You are confident and powerful. You understand that everything you need to succeed is within you NOW.

You are an amazing achiever who takes action toward your goals every single day.

You can do anything. You are filled with self-confidence.

Your confidence gives you the power to achieve anything that you desire.

You are overflowing with powerful self-confidence.

Your mind is clear and sharp at all times. You take action immediately towards your goals.

Your subconscious mind accepts all of these suggestions and they are now your reality. You are filled with an abundance of self-confidence.

You are an amazing and powerful person.

You have complete self-confidence...

(Notice that each suggestion is written in the positive and also that the theme of the suggestions are the same. They are also repetitive, which will help the primary idea and suggestion to be accepted by your subconscious mind)

(Awaken Back to Full Consciousness)

In a moment, I will count from one to five. When I reach five, you will be fully awakened, feeling more alert and awake than when we began this session. You will understand that you have done something wonderful by taking this time for yourself. You will also understand that with each session of hypnosis, you will find yourself dropping down faster and deeper than the time before. You will understand that you enjoy these sessions and that you feel completely empowered and full of enthusiasm after each one. Your subconscious mind is accepting all suggestions and you are becoming the person of your destiny.

One…starting to become more aware of your surroundings

Two…take a deep breath, and feel that energy-giving oxygen rushing through your body

Three…feel a surge of energy rushing in through your toes and up through your entire body

Four…your head washed through with fresh, cool spring water. Head clear, body clear.

And, Five…open your eyes, and wide-awake!

So there you have it, your very own self-hypnosis program. This is one of the most effective and powerful tools that you will find in this book. Whatever you do, do not skip this part. Hypnosis is truly the fastest and most powerful way to reprogram your mind from the person you used to be into the person of your chosen destiny.

If you would like to avoid going through the trouble of creating your own self-hypnosis recordings, There are many pre-made recordings available for sale on my hypnosis website at www.LiveHypnotist.com. I also offer customized, audio-hypnosis sessions. These sessions will be completely customized, and recorded by me, to match your exact leadership and destiny achieving goals. The pre-recorded audio-hypnosis sessions can also effectively help people to quit smoking, boost self confidence, lose weight, banish insomnia, and rid fears and phobias, and are available on the products page of the **LiveHypnotist.com** website. All you have to do is listen to your personal recording daily. Over time, the suggestions will become your reality.

13 THE EXTRAORDINARY POWER OF INTUITION

I find that the harder I work, the more luck I seem to
have. - Thomas Jefferson

Developing Intuition

Now that you have created a laser-like focus toward achieving your planned destiny, you will begin to feel "lucky" often. Because you now know exactly what it is that you desire, both consciously and subconsciously, you will begin to see opportunities, sometimes in the most unlikely places and from the most unlikely sources. When these opportunities present themselves, you must be willing to rely on your intuition. Your intuition is your gut-instinct, your hunches, your dreams, and that little voice inside of your head. It is your subconscious mind's way of communicating with your conscious mind.

When your intuition kicks in, now is NOT a time to hesitate. Whenever you are presented with a window of opportunity, you must act intuitively, and you must act immediately. Everything that we've talked about, so far, in this book has led us to intuition. Intuition, and the ability to control it, is the seemingly magic part of the equation that makes "predicting the future" possible.

All of us have intuitive abilities. Intuition is not some magical, supernatural power that's only available to psychics, magicians, and mentalists. It is the result of a mind that knows exactly where it needs to go in order to achieve a goal. Intuition, without focus, is fear. Intuition, with laser-like focus, is an idea that comes to you in a dream.

It's a feeling in your gut that you have to introduce yourself to that person on the elevator. It is listening, and reacting to, that voice in your mind. Not the voice of fear, but the voice of your subconscious mind. That is the voice that is going to show you the shortest route toward achieving your destiny.

> The only real valuable thing is intuition.
> I believe in intuitions and inspirations...I sometimes feel that I
> am right. I do not know that I am. - Albert Einstein

Intuition is the closest thing that I've seen to being real magic. Many of the books that I've read on the subject, claim that intuition, by way of our subconscious mind, is our connection to some ultimate force in the universe. Some call this force, Infinite Intelligence, the Universe, the Force, God, or a thousand other names. The idea is that the answer to every conceivable question exists somewhere in the universe as a form of energy. If our subconscious minds, which are supposedly our direct connection to Infinite Intelligence, can tap into that energy, then the answers will be fed back to our conscious minds through intuition. The lack of scientific based evidence to support the claim that an ultimate intelligence even exists, leaves that explanation open for debate. For our purposes, it doesn't matter exactly how or why it works anyway, only that it does indeed work. The sheer volume of books that have been written about the subject over the course of centuries, all with contrasting explanations on why it works, shows us that anyone who applies the techniques, regardless of religion, belief, race, or gender, will experience the same results.

So what does intuition feel like when it's unveiling a path toward your destiny? It feels very similar to the recollection of a lost memory. Like when you're conversing with someone and you say, "I can't remember her name, but it will come to me." Then you find that the more you try to remember the name, the more lost it becomes. It isn't until later, when you've consciously stopped trying to remember, that the name suddenly "pops" into your mind. The difference between remembering a name and intuition is that the name is something that you already knew. Intuition will often be an idea that you didn't even know existed. It will seem to come from nowhere, but it will be the exact answer that you are seeking. When it happens, and it will happen, it can be exciting, spooky, and mind-blowing all at the same time.

> I feel there are two people inside me - me and my intuition. If I go against her, she'll screw me every time, and if I follow her, we get along quite nicely.
> - Kim Basinger

Unlock The D.O.O.R. To Your Intuition At Will

Intuition may present itself to you in many forms. An idea, thought, or answer might come to you in a dream. It might come to you while you're wide-awake or maybe you'll read an article the holds the answer you've been searching for. Your job is to listen to your intuition and act on it. The techniques that you have been given throughout this book, including: properly writing your goals, actively listening to others, using powerful words, and practicing visualization and self-hypnosis, will allow intuition become your most effective, destiny building, asset. Everyone is gifted with intuitive abilities, but without extreme focus, intuition is like a rudderless boat in the sea of perpetual confusion. Because you will have created the foresight of where you want to go, you will intuitively discover the needed steps to get you there.

Over time, your ability to rely on your intuition will increase. You must allow it to work for you, and you must act on the information that it provides. If you choose to ignore its advice, it may stop supplying it. It's like a muscle that needs exercise to grow. It will be working with you, and for you, throughout your journey toward achieving your planned destiny. It will provide you with everything that you need in order to reach your goals, become a great leader, and fulfill your destiny. With practice, you will be able to call upon it at will. You will be able to find the answers to any questions or problems that you need to solve. The way to do this is something that you've probably done hundreds of times throughout your life, perhaps without even knowing it.

I have fashioned a system, or formula, that will allow you to fully activate your intuition at will. This formula is how brand new ideas, thoughts, inventions, methods, and techniques have been created throughout the ages, yet it is unknown to most. Most of us unknowingly use this formula, out of necessity, only when we're faced with a problem that brings with it a burning desire to find its solution. This could be a life or death situation, or a situation where the idea of failure is simply not an option. In those instances, we instinctively apply the formula and allow our subconscious minds and intuition to go to work.

Think back to a time when you became obsessed with solving a problem. Maybe you needed to come up with a certain amount of money, maybe you needed to invent a nonexistent widget to fix something or to make a task more efficient, or maybe you needed to find the perfect words to explain something to someone. You probably thought about it, with full-force, for a day or two. Then all of a sudden, when you least expected it and were either thinking about something else or were sound asleep, the answer just "appeared" in your mind. What if you could make that process happen every time? Well, guess what? You can!

The formula to open the door to your intuition is contained in an acronym, D.O.O.R. DOOR stands for Define, Obsess, Overwhelm, and Relax. These are the same steps that you inevitably take when you activate your intuition by instinct. Knowing that it's also possible to trigger your intuition whenever you need it will provide you with a level of power that few possess. The amount of focus that you already have in alignment with your planned destiny, will be at constant work with your subconscious mind. Even while you're asleep, your subconscious mind will be finding ways to move you closer to your planned destiny. It's like having passive income for you mind. These ideas will then be revealed to you through your intuition. Let's take a closer look at the DOOR to intuition formula.

Whenever you need an answer to a specific problem or question, or if you just need some inspiration, all you have to do is follow these steps:

D. Define the problem.

First, you must decide exactly what it is that you're trying to solve. This doesn't have to be as specific as your goal setting, but it doesn't hurt to get specific either. Do you need an invention that will solve a certain problem? Do you need to connect with a certain person, but don't know how? Do you need to find a way to fund an endeavor? It can be anything at all, really. Just make sure it's something that applies to what you're ultimately trying to accomplish.

O. Obsess over the problem.

The next step is to put your conscious mind to work. You want to look at this problem from every possible angle. Try, as hard as you can, to solve the problem on your own. Study it. Look it up online. Read about it. Ask others for help about, etc. Do this until you feel that you've exhausted all possibilities. You never know, you might just solve the problem without having to rely on intuition, but if not, move on to the next step.

O. Overwhelm your mind with the problem.

After you've gathered a boatload of information about your problem, you'll want to spend more time thinking about it. You'll want to think about it so much, that you finally reach a point of mental exhaustion. How long this takes can vary from person to person and also from problem to problem. It could be an hour or it could be two weeks. Just allow it to consume your mind until you just can't think about it anymore. Then move onto the final step.

R. Relax.

Stop thinking about the problem altogether, and just allow your mind to flow freely. I personally prefer to do this final step, right before I fall asleep at night. I'll actually stay in the Overwhelm stage while lying in bed, but as soon as I feel myself drifting off to sleep, I let go of the problem and allow my mind wander freely.

What you've done with the DOOR process is focus all of your conscious energy on solving your problem. That extreme amount of focus was preparing your subconscious mind to take over. It won't take over completely until you're willing to let go of the problem consciously. I know that this sounds counterintuitive, but think back to when you were try to remember someone's name. It never "pops" into your mind if you're trying to think of it. So, just allow your subconscious to take control, and soon, it will provide you with your answer. Go to sleep, get some exercise, read a book, or focus something else for a while. Do anything but think about your problem and allow The Law of Attraction and your intuition to take over.

Often, you have to rely on intuition. - Bill Gates

Intuition comes very close to clairvoyance; it appears to be
the extrasensory perception of reality. - Alexis Carrel

You Must Take Immediate Action On Your Intuition

Once your subconscious mind obtains the answer from the universe, or wherever else it gets it from, it will present it to you. It may come to you in a dream, or while you're awake. You might look at a painting that you've seen a thousand times, and suddenly, it will give you the perfect idea to solve your problem. Your message can come from anywhere, and in any form. Your job is to be aware when it happens, and to take immediate action on it. This is also when your listening skills will prove most useful. If you don't take prompt action, the idea might disappear from your mind forever. If you do take action on the information, your conscious and subconscious minds will be working in harmony together. The more they're working in harmony, the better you'll become at using the D.O.O.R. technique. Eventually, you'll find yourself feeling as though you have some secret super-power, and you'll want to share it with anyone who will listen. You might even decide to write a book that teaches people how to use it. See what I did there?

Many of the most useful and powerful ideas will come to you while you sleep. They may come in the form of dreams, or you might just wake up with a brand new thought. My advice for you is to always keep a pad of paper and a pencil next to your bed. As soon as you have a creative idea, write it down instantly. I can't tell you how many times I've made the mistake of not immediately writing down a thought that came to me in a dream. I woke up, and thought, "Wow, that's a great idea! I'd better write that down in the morning." Then I fall back asleep and guess what? Yup, it was never to be remembered again. Please don't do that. Write it down as soon as you think of it. If you don't want to use a pad of paper and a pencil, just quickly type something into your cell phone, or leave yourself a short voice memo. In fact, voice memos are my go-to if an idea comes while I'm not sleeping.

How powerful your intuition becomes will depend largely on your willingness to take immediate action on it, or your speed of implementation. Your intuition will show you the way, but it then becomes your conscious responsibility to see it through. It's as though intuition is the supplier of the map that will lead you to your grandest treasure. Having the map isn't the same as having the treasure. In order to reach the treasure, you must be willing to travel the course of the map, and to do that, you'll need a plan. Your business plan, or destiny plan, is where your conscious mind will take over. Now that your intuition has shown you the way to get there, you conscious mind can work on the details and the logistics of arriving. That is not to say that you will no longer require the use of your subconscious mind and intuition. You will actually be using them throughout your entire journey. They will be providing you with faster, better, and superior shortcuts along the way. They will also be there whenever a roadblock comes along to help you maintain momentum.

With practice, your conscious mind, subconscious mind, and intuition will work flawlessly together, creating a harmonious symphony that I call the leadership mentality. Consciously activating your subconscious mind, in order to call upon your intuition, will eventually become second nature. You will have the ability to tap into an infinite source of knowledge, ideas, and creativity, at will. You will understand what ancient writers meant when they wrote of things like Zen, enlightenment, or universal harmony. You will be able to utilize your mind to its fullest potential, and have the ability to conquer the destiny of your dreams often in a seemingly miraculous fashion.

14 OVERCOMING FEAR

I've had a lot of worries in my life, most of which never
happened. - Mark Twain

Fight, Flight or Freeze

The primary barrier that will stand between you and your planned
destiny, even after applying the techniques outlined in this book, is fear.
The reason that millions of people, who have all read the same success-
based books, and have the same information, fail to succeed is inaction
caused by fear. Fear causes us to procrastinate and get stuck in an
eternal phase of planning. Fear is a very powerful entity that must be
dealt with if you wish to move forward. The goal isn't to eliminate fear,
but to learn how to move past it, lessen it, or transform it to be used to
our advantage.

I've been performing and speaking on stages since the age of
fourteen. In some form or another, I believe that we all have stage
fright hardwired into our DNA. The first time I stepped onto a stage to
perform, my hands were shaking so badly that I almost couldn't hold
onto the microphone. The audience could visually see the microphone
trembling from side to side as though I was holding a vibrating
microphone. After thousands of performances, you'd think that this
fear would have passed, but guess what? It's still there. Only now if you
see me on stage you'd never know it. I was never able to eliminate the
fear. Instead, I learned how to harness it and actually turn it into an
asset. Stage fright has become the fuel that I use to energize my

presentations. It's what I've become addicted to. I believe that it is possible to transform fear, in any endeavor, into a different form of energy that's actually useful. In fact, I've even produced a book and online video course to help others conquer their fear of public speaking. For more information, visit: www.CrushStageFright.com.

First, let's talk about what fear actually is. I don't want you to think that all fear is bad. Fear is inevitable as it's part of our survival instincts. It is hard-wired into our DNA and exists because it helps to keep us safe. The problem with fear is that the oldest part of our brain, or our lizard brain, hasn't had enough time to evolve with the fast-paced changes that have occurred in society over the course of the past several thousand years. Our lizard brains do not have the ability to distinguish between actual life-threatening situations, and situations that, in modern times are quite harmless. Traditionally, fear would help our species survive by activating fight, flight or freeze sequences in times of actual danger. For example, if you were in the jungle, and you suddenly spotted a lion, your lizard brain would cause you to automatically freeze. This would not be a conscious reaction, but an automatic, subconscious one. Your chance of survival, if you held still, would increase. Those who didn't have this survival instinct might have kept on moving, and would have become lunch for the lion.

In modern times, many of the fear instincts that were necessary to keep us alive thousands of years ago, are no longer practical. Sure, it's still a good idea to freeze if you spot a lion in the jungle, but how often does that happen? For most of us, it will probably never happen. This automatic, or lizard-brain, response shows up in our lives in situations where the risk of death is essentially zero. It's basically a misfiring of the fight, flight, or freeze response. Many people claim that their biggest fear is speaking in public. So much so that the thought of speaking in public can cause people to tremble, vomit, or have anxiety attacks, but why? Does speaking in public put your life at risk? Sure, there have been times when a public speaker, such as a president, has been shot, but if you look at the number of speeches given next to the number of attempts made on a speaker's life, the risk factor is basically nil. So why does our lizard brain respond as though we're about to die when put in this type of risk-free situation? It's because our lizard brains haven't been updated to lizard brain 2.0 for thousands and thousands of years. It's as though that section of our brain is still running on DOS, while the world is running Mac OS X or the latest version of Windows.

Unfortunately, outside from taking beta-blockers, which I don't recommend for this purpose, we cannot do a software update on our lizard brains. Instead, we need to adjust to it and find ways to manipulate it. We need to build workaround software in our minds that can leverage the fight, flight or freeze responses and use them to our benefit. There are several ways to do this including preparation, practice, visualization, and changing your expectations. If you use these techniques, fear will eventually become your friend. It will no longer be something that holds you back, but will instead become the rocket-fuel that you will use to propel yourself, with lightning speed, toward achieving your planned destiny. Also, because fear lives in our subconscious minds, hypnosis can be used to change your fear paradigm.

> If you are willing to do only what's easy, life will be
> hard. But if you're willing to do what's hard, life will be
> easy. -T. Harv Eker

Fear Transformation Techniques

Preparation: The first way to control fear is by being prepared. Regardless of whether you're getting ready to deliver a speech, approach an attractive person in a bar, make a cold call, or deliver a sales pitch, preparation is vital if you want to suppress or control fear. Going into an endeavor without a plan of action, will increase fear and anxiety. But, if you know exactly what you're going to say and do, and also how you're going to respond to all of the possible responses from the other person or persons, your level of fear will diminish.

Think of yourself like a football coach who's getting ready to coach his team in the Super Bowl. Successful teams spend a tremendous amount of time on preparation. They study countless hours of video of their opponent's past performances. They design a complete action plan for the game, complete with flexible alternatives in case things don't go as expected. They make sure the players are well rehearsed in all of their plays. They make sure the team is well rested, well fed, and as injury free as possible. Weeks, days, and countless hours are spent in preparation for a single game. Do they still feel fear? Of course they do, but not nearly as much as if they hadn't prepared to their full potential. The more prepared you are for any situation, the more confident you will be in your ability to perform. Confidence is an enemy of fear, so the more confidence you can accumulate, the better.

There comes a point where preparation can actually become a hindrance to your success. There are many people who spend an entire lifetime "preparing" to do something big, but they never actually take action on it. Don't allow preparation to become an excuse to avoid facing your fears. Preparation is not something to hide behind, and must not be used as an excuse for procrastination. The easiest way to avoid falling into the trap of using preparation as an excuse to not take action, is to set deadlines. Don't prepare for a meeting that doesn't yet exist with the plan of scheduling the meeting when you're ready. Instead, plan the meeting first. This is an incredibly useful tactic that will force you into action. It's been called the "Ready, Fire, Aim" approach, and it works wonderfully.

An example from my personal experience comes from hypnosis. After I became certified as a stage hypnotist, I failed to actually perform a single hypnosis show for two full years. I kept telling myself that I'd book a hypnosis show as soon as my show was fully prepared, and perfected. In the meantime, I was fine speaking on leadership and performing mentalism shows because I was already used to doing those. For some reason, I had a fear of actually performing a live hypnosis show. What if nobody went under? What if I looked like a fool? And so I used preparation as an excuse not to take action. Eventually, my hypnosis coach reminded me of the Ready, Fire, Aim principle and said that in order to break my cycle of procrastination, I needed to book the show first. So that's what I did. I booked a show, two months out, and then spent those next two months preparing as much as possible, but this time with a deadline. It worked perfectly. The show was an outstanding success and I was awarded with an entirely new stream of opportunities. If it hadn't been for my coach, I might still be preparing today and would have let thousands of performance opportunities slip through my fingers.

Visualization:

The next way to manipulate fear is through visualization. Fear tends to reveal its ugly head whenever we're doing something for the first time. Even with preparation, the fear of the unknown can make us feel uneasy, anxious, and nervous about an event that's about to occur. Visualization can help alleviate those feelings. The more exposed we become to a given situation, the more comfortable and relaxed we become.

As I mentioned in the chapter on visualization, our subconscious minds cannot tell the difference between an actual occurrence and an occurrence that is properly visualized. Knowing this will allow you to experience a scenario in your mind multiple times before it actually occurs in real life. This is why professional athletes will actively visualize themselves playing the perfect game or match, over and over again, before the real deal comes. I use this technique before speaking to groups. First, I'll look up the venue online, if I haven't been there before, and try to find a picture of the presentation room. Then I'll use that image to visualize myself onstage, delivering the perfect speech to a wonderful and appreciative audience. Then, on the day of the event, I'll show up to the venue early enough that I have the room to myself. I'll then stand on the stage, and again visualize the presentation going exactly as planned in my mind. Once the emcee is introducing me, in real life, my mind is at ease because, as far as it knows, I've already delivered this presentation a hundred times. This can be applied to any situation that you associate with feelings of fear. Give it a try, and I'm certain that you'll never go without it.

Practice:

Visualization is a great way to convince your mind that you've already experience a situation before it actually happens. That being said, it is even more powerful to snuff out fear by actually practicing an act over and over.

It goes without saying that, the more you do something, the easier it becomes. If your fear happens to be cold calling, and cold calling happens to be an essential part of reaching your planned destiny, then do it as much as possible. Sticking with the cold calling example, a great way to get in as much practice as possible is to go for numbers. Don't focus on making sales or connections so much in the beginning. Just pick up the phone and call a given number of people everyday, and don't care one bit about the outcome of those calls. Make it your goal to get 100 people in a week to say "No" to you. Eventually, the fear that you once felt when picking up the phone, will change into another form of energy known as excitement.

You might still feel nervous, but you will learn through experience and repetition, that calling people is not a life-threatening activity. You will eventually be able to turn the fight, flight, or freeze response into excitement as though you're participating in a game that gives you a positive rush of energy.

The great thing about practice is that it doesn't even have to be with the specific task that you fear. Anytime you force yourself to step out of your comfort zone, your comfort zone will begin to expand in all areas of your life. Like leadership, your comfort zone is never static. It is either expanding or contracting, so you must make a conscious effort to make sure it is constantly expanding.

They say that your success in life is in direct proportion to the size of your comfort zone, so work to make it as large as possible. Expanding your comfort zone will make you feel uncomfortable, but keep in mind that when you are uncomfortable, you are growing. It's like lifting weights. A certain amount of weight will feel uncomfortable at first, but as your muscles adjust, recover, and grow, that same weight eventually becomes easy and you can move on toward conquering weights that would have previously been impossible to lift.

In your office, on your bedroom mirror, or somewhere that you will see it daily, hang the phrase, "I do at least one thing EVERY DAY that scares me." Then hold yourself accountable and do it. If you see that sign at the end of the day, don't allow yourself to go to sleep until you do something that will expand your comfort zone. If you get into the habit of doing one thing that scares you at the beginning of each day, I promise you that you will feel unstoppable for the rest of that entire day. There are endless things that you can do to expand your comfort zone. Take an improv or acting class, for example. You'll learn how to think on your feet, and how to be bold in front of total strangers. Take a dance class, sing a song at a karaoke bar, volunteer to speak at your local chamber of commerce, or sign up for martial arts classes.

There are millions of things that can help you expand your comfort zone. You can also force yourself to do something that actually is dangerous and scary. Go skydiving, scuba dive with sharks, or go bungee jumping. Having these types of experiences will help you to view less threatening fears as just that. How scary can making a phone call be after you've survived jumping out of an airplane at 10,000 feet? Positive side effects that often come along with forcing yourself to experience new things are that you will automatically become a more creative person and you might also discover a missing piece of your destiny puzzle along the way.

Change your expectations:

By changing your state of mind, when entering into a feared activity, you can take the self-inflicted pressure off of yourself and ease your fear. For this technique, let's use making a sales call as our example. If your state of mind going into the call is that you must make the sale in order to reach your goals, then your level of fear will rise. Instead of going into the call with an "I must succeed" attitude, try going at it with a sense of sharing. If your mindset is "How can I help this person achieve his or her goals," instead of "How will this help me achieve my goals," your lizard brain will not trigger the unwanted nervous response.

When coming from a place of giving, there is no need for fear to appear. If I gave you a million dollars and said to start calling random people out of the phone book to give the money too, would you feel any fear at all? I'm guessing not. That's because giving is not a selfish act. If you can convince your mind that your sales call is also an unselfish act, that has the potential client's best interest in mind, you will have no reason to feel fear. Practice changing fear into a feeling of "I can't wait to show this person how much I can make his or her life easier," and your fear will disappear. It's simply a matter of consciously changing your perspective on the activity at hand.

My favorite example on how effective it is to simply change your perspective, belief or paradigm of a situation comes from the world of running. Until 1954, no one had been able to run a mile in under four minutes. In fact, most believed that it was simply impossible and that the human body was incapable of ever doing it. They believed that the human body would completely shut down and collapse before it could achieve that goal. This limiting belief was so widely accepted, that runners even stopped trying it. That was until Roger Bannister proved everyone wrong by achieving that exact goal. Forty-six days after Bannister ran a mile in under four minutes, another runner actually beat his time. In the next few years after Bannister's accomplishment, several other runners were able to do the same. What you believe has tremendous power, and if you believe that you can move past fear…you can.

> Knowing that my habits of thought become the patterns which attract all the circumstances affecting my life through the lapse of Time, I shall keep my mind so busy in connection with the circumstances I desire that no Time will be left to devote to fears and frustrations, and the things I do not desire. - Napoleon Hill

Too Focused To Be Afraid

> Inaction breeds doubt and fear. Action breeds confidence and courage. If you want to conquer fear, do not sit home and think about it. Go out and get busy. - Dale Carnegie

As mentioned in the quote above, it is also possible to diminish, or even extinguish, fear by having no time for it. After you have been applying the techniques in this book, and your conscious and subconscious minds are congruent towards a single goal or destiny, you won't have time to be afraid. Fear tends to creep in during times of uncertainty. But, when you're going after your destiny with everything in your being, fear will be left in the dust.

A useful tactic to keep fear at bay is to schedule your day the night before, everyday. Get yourself a daily planner, either a paper one or find an app, and then schedule your entire day down to the minute. Set aside time to work on achieving your mini-goals, time for your family, time for exercise, affirmations, etc. The key is NOT to leave any access time for fear. If you know, because it's on your planner, that you must make ten phone calls between 9:00 am and 9:30 am, you'll just get to it. Because it's part of your schedule, there won't be any time to allow fear, anxiety, or worry to build up. Removing that extra "fear-building" time will enable you to just act. Just start DOING immediately. If you hesitate for more than a few seconds, your imagination will begin to think of all of the things that might go wrong, but if you jump right in, you can skip that unneeded rush of adrenaline altogether. Mel Robbins wrote a fantastic book about not hesitating before taking an otherwise fearful action called "The 5 Second Rule." It's a great read and I highly recommend it. You can also find Mel Robbins' TED Talk on the subject by searching YouTube. It's a great video to give you a kick in the butt whenever it's needed.

If you try the fear removing techniques in this chapter, but find yourself stuck with certain actions that you just can't seem to push past, you might want to try applying the affirmations and self-hypnosis techniques, discussed previously, to your fear. By telling yourself over and over that you love to speak on stage, for example, or by reprogramming your subconscious mind through hypnosis to believe that you love speaking or cold calling, you will eventually find that belief as being accepted. Even if it's not fully accepted, you will find that the power of the fear will be diminished dramatically. At the end of the day, it is fear that prevents most people from reaching their full potential. Do not allow fear, which is almost always no more than a meaningless thought, to control your life. Push through it, go around it, or squash it like a bug. It is not your friend and it would like nothing more than to see you fail. So, decide here and now that fear will never be an acceptable excuse for any of your destiny achieving efforts.

15 OWNING THE STAGE:
THE POWER OF PUBLIC SPEAKING
AND WHY IT'S ESSENTIAL TO YOUR SUCCESS

> ...Speaking in front of a crowd is the number one fear of the average person...Number two was death...This means to the average person, if you have to be at a funeral, you would rather be in the casket than doing the eulogy. - Jerry Seinfeld

There is a direct correlation between a person's ability to confidently speak in public and the speed at which they achieve success. Those who speak will also tend to make more money than those who don't. If you happen to be in the 90 percentile of people who would rather die than speak in public, it's time to conquer that fear. Even if you don't have a fear of public speaking, you're bound to find a few useful tips in this chapter that will raise your speaking skills to new heights, so read on.

The ability to speak in public can have a formidable impact on how fast you're able to reach your predetermined destiny. Even if your quest doesn't seem to involve you ever having to stand on a stage and speak, there are other forms of communication where mastering this skill will be essential. Speaking during sales meetings, at networking events, during webinars, on television, radio, at conferences, and newspaper interviews, and at seminars are important areas where speaking confidence is a must. Speaking is everywhere. In today's day and age, much of our marketing might be through social media like Facebook Live, YouTube, Instagram, Snapchat or whatever social media is popular when you're reading this. In order to build a tribe of followers, who can help you to achieve your goals faster, you must communicate with them and that always involves public speaking.

Other reasons to master the skill of public speaking include but are not limited to:

- Speaking is the most effective way to get you message out to the world
- It allows you to be seen as THE expert in your field
- It makes you more visible and memorable to the public and your organization
- Confident speaking is viewed as an important leadership quality
- It enables you to clarify your message
- Speaking causes potential partners to reach out and contact you (Instead of the other way around)
- It builds your self-confidence for all social situations
- It's the best way to generate more sales
- It generates a platform for you to build your tribe
- Speakers tend to get promotions faster
- It enables you to bring about change in your community
- It gives you the ability to inform, persuade, and entertain

A side bonus that comes along with speaking in public is that you just might fall in love with it as I have. The feeling that you get before stepping onto a stage can become absolutely addictive. I've jumped out of perfectly good airplanes, scuba dived with sharks (several times), and bungee jumped off of a bridge, but nothing can compare to the positive rush of energy that an audience of a thousand people can provide. Those of you who already speak probably know what I mean. Those who don't are likely starting to feel a bit uneasy right now. Don't worry, you're not alone. I was once where you are, but I found ways to completely transform my stage fright into what I like to call "Stage Might," and you can too!

If you suffer from stage fright, then you know that it can be the worst feeling in the world. Your body trembles, your voice cracks, and you just want to crawl under a rock and die. So why bother putting yourself in that situation in the first place? The short answer is massive financial gain. The long answer is so that you can build your tribe of followers who will help you in the achievement of your destiny. I know it doesn't seem fair especially if you happen to have been cursed with stage fright, but I'm not the one who made up the rules, so don't blame me. It's just the way things are. That being said, I'm about to provide you with everything that I've learned in the past 20 years as a professional speaker and entertainer about conquering stage fright. This information was taken from my book and video course called **"Crush Stage Fright."** I'll also cover some really useful tips that will help take your speaking effectiveness to the next level.

> There are only two types of speakers in the world. 1. The
> nervous and 2. Liars. - Mark Twain

How To Speak Confidently On Any Stage…Even If You Have Stage Fright

So, what can you do to stop allowing the fear of public speaking to limit your income potential? The good news is that you are not alone. In fact, most of the successful public speakers, even the best of the best, have had to deal with stage fright in one form or another. Some of them still deal with it everyday.

Stage fright isn't unique to you. It's actually pretty much universal. Sure, some have it more than others, but the truth is that stage fright is simply a misfiring of the fight or flight response as we talked about earlier. It's your brain telling you that you're approaching a life-threatening situation when in reality you are not. Our society has evolved extremely fast throughout the past several thousand years, but our brains failed to keep pace in some respects. Back when humans lived in tribal communities, speaking in public may have actually been a life-threatening endeavor. Anger the tribe, or the tribe of your enemy, by speaking out and you might have risked execution or possibly exclusion from the tribe, which back then would have actually been dangerous.

Nowadays, speaking in public carries almost no life-threatening risk, but your brain doesn't know that. So, it freaks out and sends a massive amount of unnecessary adrenaline rushing through your body. The result is that you're left with enough energy to slay a lion, or at least run from one, and you're trying to contain all of that energy while standing still. It has to leak out somewhere and ends up making you look like a nervous wreck. So what can you do to avoid that response?

Avoiding that response is actually the wrong thing to attempt and that's why so many "would be" speakers fail. The real secret is not to try and stop the fight, flight or freeze response, but to embrace it. Stopping it all together simply doesn't work. Sure, you can learn to lessen your body's reaction with practice, hypnosis, and other methods that we'll cover shortly. But, you can never completely erase it, and trust me, you don't want to erase it! How do I know this? Ask any top level speaker if they get a rush of adrenaline before they walk on stage and 99% will tell you yes. You see, it's not that they've learned how to avoid stage fright, it's that they've learned how to manipulate it to their benefit.

Rather than seeing pre-talk nervousness as pre-talk terror, they see it as a pre-talk rush of positive-excitement. All that's required to pull this off is a switch in your mentality…and a little practice as well. The next time you're about to speak in public, just remind yourself that the feelings you're experiencing are not your own. They are coming from the reptilian part of your brain, which is a part of your brain that every human has. It is not YOU that is nervous, it is only the part of your brain that is stuck in the past. Stuck thousands of years in the past to be more specific. The first step to take is to reframe your approach to public speaking. For now on, stop thinking, "I can't believe I HAVE to do this." Instead, reframe that thought into, "I can't believe I GET to do this!" I know it sounds simple, but this single step can work wonders towards building your onstage confidence.

There are many tips, tricks, and techniques that make accomplishing this mind-shift easier, faster, and more effective. As mentioned before, I've written an entire book about the subject, but for now, I'm going to give you the most effective techniques that I have been personally using on stages for the past 20-years.

> It usually takes me more than three weeks to prepare a good impromptu speech. - Mark Twain

Insider Speaking Secrets

A large part of easing stage fright comes from being well prepared. So what exactly does that mean when applied towards speaking? Preparing to give a speech, a short talk, deliver a webinar presentation, or even an elevator pitch, begins with knowing your desired endgame. What is the purpose of your talk? What is it that you wish to accomplish by speaking? Once you know where you want to end up, you can work backwards from there to design your perfect presentation. By knowing where you want to go, you've already taken a bit of the anxiety away because you are speaking with a purpose. Then you must learn your material inside and out. If you're speaking about something that coincides with a goal that you wish to achieve, you will be speaking from a point of passion and this will automatically improve your performance.

I once heard someone say that, "Confidence is knowing your lines." I can't remember who said it. It might have been George Burns, but it doesn't seem to show up anywhere on Google. Anyway, that phrase has always stuck in my mind because it's so true. When you know your topic inside and out, your confidence will be greatly enhanced. You won't be worried about messing up or receiving a tough question from the audience because you know your material better than anyone else. You are the expert on your topic. Or at least, you are the expert on your speech. When writing your speech, it is much easier to utilize bullet points as opposed to writing out the speech word for word. When you write out every single line of a speech, it can come off as robotic to the audience. Plus, memorizing a word for word speech is much more difficult. If you happen to lose your place, you will surely feel a huge rush of panic set in. First knowing your topic well, and using bullet points can easily avoid this panic. This method also allows you to be flexible during the presentation. Once on stage, unpredictable things will happen. A waiter might drop a dish, someone might ask a question, or the microphone might stop working. If you're locked into a memorized speech, these things can really throw you off. But, by using bullet points, or an outline of your speech, you will be able to acknowledge the unplanned incident and then quickly get back on track.

I'm not suggesting that you should never write out a speech word for word. In fact, I do just that. I'll first write an outline with an introduction, followed by the main topics and the key points that I want to cover on each topic, and then the conclusion. I'll read this over and over, but when I actually practice delivering the speech, I don't worry about getting it right word for word. All that I care about is that I hit each main topic and the key points that I wish to cover. If you know your topic as well as you should, your outline should be enough for you to talk about each point because you already know what it is that you wish to convey. So, do you have to memorize the outline? Well, yes and no. With enough rehearsal, you will find yourself automatically remembering the outline, including all of the key points, bits of information, stories, and even jokes that you wish to include. If you really want to commit the outline to memory, you can use a memory technique called linking. Actually, there are several memory techniques that you could use, but again, that's another book in itself, so we'll stick to linking for now.

How to Use the Linking Memory Technique for Speeches:

If you're not familiar with linking, here's a quick tutorial. The way that our memories work best is by using pictures. Actual words don't mean anything to our minds, but pictures do. Words are intangible symbols that we have to translate into meaning, but pictures are real at least to our minds. Also, our minds tend to more easily remember pictures that are unusual, frightening or gross. So what we're going to do is go through your outline and turn each topic and key point into a picture.

Let's say, for example, that your first topic is how to make a peanut butter and jelly sandwich. A strange topic, I know, but I happen to be hungry right now and that sounds delicious. So what we're going to do is look at the key topics in our speech, turn them into pictures, and then link them together, like a chain, in an unusual way. Let's say that we want to cover 1. Bread selection, 2. Peanut Butter selection, 3. Jelly selection, and 4. How to make the sandwich. What we'll do is start with bread.

Imagine a giant piece of your favorite kind of bread. The reason we're making it giant is because our brain will remember it more easily if we make our picture strange, unusual, violent, or disturbing. When doing this exercise on your own, you will want to activate your imagination to come up with your own unusual mental picture. Now, we need to somehow visually link that giant piece of bread to the next thing on our outline, which in our case is the peanut butter. Let's imagine a thousand tiny jars of peanut butter, with arms and legs, running around the giant piece of bread, trying to attack it by spitting peanuts at the bread. Yes, I realize how weird this seems, but trust me, the more weird it is, the better. When you're picturing this in your mind, it's important to make it feel real. Imagine that you're actually witnessing this event happen. Imagine the details of the occurrence. What sounds do you hear, what does it smell like, etc.? Make it feel as real as possible. Feeling the emotions that you might actually feel if you really witnessed this event will lock it into your memory. Next, we need to link the peanut butter to the jelly. Of course in this example, the two obviously go together anyway, but this will work with any and all topics as long as you're able to turn each one into a picture in your mind. Let's imagine that you love peanut butter (my apologies to those who might be allergic). You might imagine running up to the peanut butter jars that are attacking the giant bread and opening jar after jar of peanut butter only to find that each jar contains nothing but jelly. Imagine that when you open them, the jelly explodes onto your face, making your face messy and sticky. Imagine how frustrating this would be so that you connect the emotion to the imagery. Finally, imagine that the only way to remove the jelly from your face is to scrape it off with a giant knife that's almost too heavy to lift. See yourself trying and feel the frustration of attempting this with a 50lb butter knife.

The linkage would look like this: Bread <-> Peanut Butter <-> Jelly <-> Knife

Now, all you have to do is go through that story in your mind during your speech. Don't worry about having to stop and "try" to remember it. If you truly visualized this story the first time around, and you attached emotions to it, it will be nearly impossible to ever forget. In fact, you'll probably have peanut butter and jelly nightmares tonight. Sorry about that in advance.

One of the most common questions that I get is what happens if I forget the very first link in the story? Well, then you're screwed. Just kidding. While it is true that not being able to remember the first linked item will cause the rest not to trigger, there is an out. The out is not to start your linked story with the first item in your speech, but instead to link it to an outside item that you're guaranteed to remember. An example of this would be to use a microphone, unless you'll be speaking without a microphone, then you'll want to choose something else. If you are using a microphone, just link the mic to the bread. For example, you could imagine that as soon as you start speaking, your microphone turns into a soggy piece of bread that's falling apart in your hands. Imagine actually feeling this soggy bread oozing between your fingers. Then, the bread begins to grow into a giant piece of bread, and in comes the peanut butter. Make sense? I would recommend keeping a short description of your linked story on a notecard. You can glance over it right before you walk on stage, but the only thing you really need to remember at that moment is the microphone. And fortunately, you will literally come face to face with a microphone the moment you step on stage.

Still feel like you need a safety net to remember your speech? Lucky for you, I have a few more cheats up my sleeve. While I always use the linking technique, I also apply these other cheats. The interesting thing is that in doing all of this preparation, you'll tend to find yourself not even needing to use them. Simply by going through the preparation and memorization process, you will become so confident in yourself that, most of the time, your memory will actually reveal all of the information that you need naturally. So let's look at some more public speaking cheats, shall we?

Speech Memory Cheats

There are several tips and tricks that professional speakers, musicians, and entertainers use to make their lives on stage much easier. As a teenage magician, I had dozens of secret techniques that would allow me to cheat on tests in high school. I know, I know, but don't hate me until I finish the story. There are many ways, especially for a magician, to secretly hide information, and then stealthily glimpse that information without being noticed by teachers or audience members.

Instead of studying for tests, I would spend hours making up these tiny little cheat sheets that could magically hide in plain site. One example that I created was to take a grey colored pen and write on it with a very fine pencil. The writing would be so small that no one could possibly notice the writing unless they had been told that it was there, and even then they'd have to look very closely. Plus, I would write the information using only the phonetic alphabet. That allowed me to put much more information in a small space, and it also made reading the information difficult for anyone not familiar with the code. The plan was to simply set this pen on my desk and read off the information. I could pick up the pen and spin it to find something written on the back. To anyone watching, it would appear as though I was simply fidgeting with the pen. The plan, if I were ever to get caught, was to simply push the pen through my fist. That would wipe off most of the lead making the information completely indecipherable.

Now before you judge me for being a cheat, let me clarify that I had only "intended" on using these items. I actually never did use them because I never needed to. As it turns out, in creating them, I was actually committing the information to memory. I was studying and didn't even know it. I guess that the fact that I was doing something sneaky and magical made it more fun for me than the thought of studying for the sake of studying.

Here are several ways that you can use to create your own on-stage cheat sheets. You can use all of them, some of them, or none of them. I like to use two or more just for the sake of boosting my onstage confidence. Just like in high school, I usually don't need to rely on any of them, but just knowing they're there is one less thing you have to worry about.

First, let's talk about using the phonetic alphabet to make your cheat sheet writing as small as possible. To utilize this easy to master technique, the first step is to remove all vowels. You generally won't need A, E, I, O, or U at all. Then you simply write each word using only the basic sounds of the consonants. This technique is also very useful when you're at a seminar and you want to take notes very quickly. In fact, I first learned of this writing technique from a course on speed-note-taking.

Examples of phonetically shortened words:
Chair would become: chr
Suitcase would become: stcs
Intuition would become: ntitn (Ok, so I used a vowel there. Sometimes it helps)
Presidential would become: prsdntl

112

As you can see, using this technique not only shortens the words by quite a bit, but it also makes it ineligible to someone not in the know. Not that it would matter if someone else could read it, unless you're a magician and it happens to be top secret information. I speak from experience here. Keep in mind that it's more important for the coding to make sense to you. Don't feel like you have to keep the writing exactly phonetic. As you can see above, I chose to include a vowel in the code for the word intuition because it would have otherwise been difficult to remember what the heck I meant to write. Now, here are some ways to apply your new stealth writing technique.

The stage version of the grey pen:

If you're going to be speaking in a context where having a marker in your hand would make sense, this is an excellent ninja cheat. All you have to do is type you mini-outline into a word processor. Make sure the lettering is large enough for your eyes to read at a distance of about 2 feet away. Minimize the spacing as much as possible and shrink the font down as small as you can without making the words too difficult to read. Print this out on a piece of paper, and then cut out a small square of the paper containing the words with a pair of scissors. You should be left with about a one-inch by one-inch square or rectangle. It could certainly be wider if needed. Then take a thick marker, perhaps one that you'll be using during your presentation on a dry-erase board, and tape the paper to the marker. I use clear cellophane tape. You'll want to tape over the entire paper, not just the edges, because the sweat on your hand will cause the ink to smear. And there you go. You now have your entire speech outline either resting in your pocket or in your hand for easy retrieval when needed.

When taking a peek on your ninja cheat sheet, you don't want to make it obvious to the audience. I've found that the best time to sneak a peak is when you are taking a moment to "think" before your next sentence. Just simply pause, and look down at the pen, as though you're thinking about something. This only takes a second and will look natural if done right. When rehearsing your speech, practice looking at the pen in a very natural way.

The microphone cheat sheet:

This one is great if you're the only one speaking at the event, or if you're the only one who will be using a particular microphone. Like we did with the marker, you will make a small version of your outline in a word-processing document or in a photo editing software like Photoshop. You'll be able to make this larger than the marker version because of the bigger size of a typical microphone. The main difference here is that you will want to make the writing a grey color and the background black. When this is taped to the microphone, it will be invisible from only a few feet away. Yet, whenever the need arises, you can simply look down at the microphone to see your next topic. I use this often when performing stage hypnosis shows. I have dozens of different hypnotic comedy routines and they're hard to keep track of because I always change them up to fit a given audience. Again, you'll want to practice looking at the microphone in a natural way. Be sure not to look too long or it will appear strange to the audience.

Other micro-cheat sheet options:

These mini-cheat sheets can be placed on anything that will naturally be in the staging area, on the back of a visual prop, or on your person. You can stick them on a water bottle, on your watch (if on your watch, be very careful to appear natural when peeking or it will look like you're bored and wondering when this will be over!), or on the outside or inside of a coffee cup. If inside the coffee cup, the cup should be empty and you should only pretend that it's full. If your speech incorporates a PowerPoint or Keynote presentation, you could also tape one of these crib sheets to the back of the remote control or just use the presenter notes.

Full sized cheat sheets:

If you have a hard time reading tiny writing, don't worry, there are larger solutions available as well. Many musicians and bands will write out their set list on one or two full-sized pieces of paper and tape them on the floor at the front of the stage. A similar option is to tape them on a floor monitor that's facing you. These are very easy to sneak a peek at, but work best on an elevated stage. If you're on the same level as the audience, using the sound monitors can still work, but I wouldn't recommend taping them onto the floor, as the audience might be able to see them. Comedians often have a bar stool on stage while they perform. The audience thinks that this is there in case the comic wants to sit down, or as a place to set their glass of water. In reality, many comedians have their entire joke list sitting right on that stool. You can do the same with a stool, a small table, or a chair. Just set a bottle or glass of water on the table as well. That way anytime you need to take a peak, just take a sip of water and the audience won't have the slightest clue of your sneaky maneuver. If the stage is black and you're going to put the sheet on the floor, you can use black construction paper and a white pen. A podium can be used as well; just don't fall into the trap of standing behind the podium and reading your entire speech off of the paper. That just looks bad and you might lose the audience's interest.

Electronic Cheat Sheets:

Finally, there are electrical cheat sheets that many speakers utilize. When delivering PowerPoint or Keynote presentations, the speakers will have their laptops in a location that's easily viewable. Those applications allow you to provide yourself with notes that the audience cannot see. And the best part is that it's operated by remote control. The scary thing about relying only on technology is that they sometimes fail. If that happens, you'll be thanking me that you also had your paper cheat sheets as backups!

Pre-Speech Rituals

Now that you no longer have to stress about memorizing your speech, we can move on to other techniques that will help you conquer stage fright. Professional athletes, Olympians, entertainers, and yes, speakers create pre-show rituals to help them get into the right state of mind, or

"The Zone." We're going to talk about several that I use and several that others have shared with me over the years. Ultimately, you will want to create your own as getting "stage ready" is different for everyone. Your pre-speech ritual will actually begin several weeks before the big day. That's when you will be practicing, remembering, and rehearsing your speech. This isn't something that you'll want to put off until the last minute unless you actually enjoy feeling like you're going to puke just before stepping on stage. Here is a list of techniques that others and myself use to get into the speaking zone.

Leading Up to The Big Day

On the days leading up to the event, make sure to get plenty of exercise, sleep, water, and healthy foods. Being well rested and hydrated will have you looking your best and will keep your voice strong. Avoid alcohol, as that tends to roughen and tire the voice. In your exercise regimen, be sure to include some form of stretching. Yoga is what I prefer, but any kind of stretching will be beneficial. This will help your blood to circulate and help you to relax while on stage. Healthy foods, especially fresh fruits and vegetables, will help supply your body with sustainable energy while speaking. On the day of the show especially, avoid refined sugars as they can cause you to crash and will actually raise stage fright levels and can cause your stomach to feel uneasy.

Avoid Caffeine!

Unless you're used to speaking regularly, do not drink coffee several hours before giving your presentation. I love coffee, but it is not your friend when it comes to delivering a presentation especially if you have stage fright. It will make your mouth dry, which can affect your voice, your throat, and your breath. Coffee can magnify your nervousness a hundred times and cause your hands and knees to shake excessively. Also, if you have too much caffeine before going onstage, your body can begin to sweat abnormally. Nothing cries "The speaker is a nervous wreck" like having sweat drip down your face when all you're doing is standing still and talking.

Use Visualization

Visualize yourself delivering the perfect speech. If it works for professional athletes, it can work for you too right? Imagine going through every line and every gesture. Also, imagine possible scenarios where things go wrong. Envision the lights going out, your hands shaking, or you stumbling on a word. Then picture yourself handling each of these events successfully. Once they've already happened in your mind, you won't be surprised if they happen in real life and you'll already know how to handle them with ease. You don't have to stress about making sure nothing ever goes wrong. Things sometimes do go wrong, even for the best speakers in the world. What matters is how well you're able to handle those situations and turn them into wins.

Just Breathe

When waiting to take the stage, take some slow, deep breaths. Deep breathing is one of the most effective ways to relax your body and your mind. While doing this, tell yourself that you love the audience. In your mind, don't make this moment about you. Make it about the wonderful experience you're about to give the audience. Don't think that the audience is going to judge you. Instead, think that you and the audience are going to have a great time together. This paradigm shift is really powerful, so don't skimp out on it.

Empty Your Mind

Stop thinking about your speech about 30-minutes before you take the stage. You've already put in the work, so if you don't know it by now, it's too late. Take this time to relax your mind and think about something completely different. If possible, strike up a conversation with people in the audience or someone backstage. If you allow yourself to dwell in your fear, it will continue to grow. So, just let it go for now. It is what it is. You're going to speak and it's going to be awesome, right? When I'm backstage, if there's no one to talk to, I juggle. Sounds strange right? But there's a reason for it. Juggling is one of the few activities that require the full attention of both sides of your brain at the same time. Juggling for me is like a form of meditation. It forces me not to think about what I'm about to do. Plus, it gets my blood flowing, makes me feel balanced, burns up some of that excess energy, and it's fun. Of course, I only juggle if I'm backstage where the audience can't see me. Otherwise that would look pretty strange. I've actually taught myself how to juggle five balls just by spending time practicing before presentations. If you want to try juggling yourself, start with three juggling beanbags. Don't use balls backstage because they can roll around and get lost, or even roll out onto the stage if you drop them. Bean bags will fall and stop. There are plenty of free tutorials available on YouTube to get you started.

Power Moves

At 10 to 15-minutes before your presentation, if you're starting to feel the effects of stage fright, do a power move. By power move, I mean do something that would normally give you a rush of energy. I'm often seen backstage shadow-boxing the curtains. Yes, I know, it's another thing that looks strange. But, I don't care at that moment. I'm taking the excess energy that's building up and releasing some of it before stepping on stage. While I'm shadow boxing, I'm actually visualizing being in a real fight. I'm trying to get my adrenaline get as high as possible. If I can get it high enough, when I walk onstage it will actually be a relaxing experience compared to what I just felt. For you, it might be remembering a time when you sacked the quarterback, won a race, or any other memory where you felt completely pumped up and elated. Interestingly, I also use this technique when I don't feel anxious enough before a presentation. After performing thousands of times, you'll have speeches where the nervousness isn't there at all, and that's not a good thing. If you feel completely calm before going on stage, your performance might lack the power that it needs to drive the audience. In those cases, your power move can be used just before walking out to raise your energy level. Why raise your energy level after you're finally calm for the first time on stage? You want to have a level of energy that's at least slightly above the audience's, because energy is contagious and you don't want your audience falling asleep.

Smile!

When you take the stage, smile right away. First impressions are everything and a smile goes a long way to getting the audience on your side. In order to make your smile genuine, think of something funny as you walk out. You also don't want to start speaking the moment you come out. Wait until you reach the center of the stage, smile, and then pause for a brief moment. This gives the audience a chance to acknowledge your presence and allows them to focus their attention. Plus, it keeps you from looking desperate for their approval. This is your talk, and you'll begin when you are ready.

Get Them On Your Side With Laughter

If possible, and appropriate for the event, always try to get a laugh at the beginning of your speech. This could be from a joke or from an observation about the audience or the event. By allowing the audience to laugh at the beginning, it will ease their tension and yours as well. Hearing the audience laugh with you can instantly melt away your anxiety. Plus it helps the audience to bond with you and with each other as you're having a shared experience. It also shows them right away that this will not be a boring presentation. I've never seen a world-class speaker who didn't use at least some humor in their presentation. You don't have to be a comedian, but a laugh here and there can be a powerful tool in your speaking arsenal.

Level the Playing Field

If you are out of your comfort zone while speaking, it can be helpful to get the audience out of theirs as well. Many speakers, including myself, will utilize techniques that are designed to make the audience take some type of physical action. It can be as simple as asking the audience to turn and find someone standing near them, whom they don't know, and introduce themselves. Or, it can be as complex as making the audience members turn to their neighbors and scream affirmations at each other as Tony Robbins does with amazing success. Robbins gets the audience out of their comfort zones and keeps them there for a full five hours or more! It's exhilarating and very effective. These kinds of tactics are a great way to keep the audience engaged, awake, and focused. In my mentalism show, the first thing I do is tell the audience that I'm going to ask them to step out of their comfort zones throughout the duration of the presentation. At first they're usually apprehensive, but by the end of the show, they're all in.

The Elephant in the Room

Unpredictable things will happen during your show and you don't need to ignore them. If someone drops something, or the microphone squeals, don't panic. I see a lot of rookie speakers try to ignore the elephant in the room, but this comes off as awkward to the audience. If something happens, don't be afraid to call attention to it, and then quickly move on with your speech. This let's the audience know that you're aware of whatever the situation is. When they see that it doesn't bother you, it won't bother them either and their attention will be back on you.

Another example of acknowledging the elephant in the room is your personal appearance. If you happen to be bald, overweight, funny looking, or whatever, call attention to it in the beginning of your presentation. For example, if you're bald like me, you may want to make a joke about it. In my speeches, after a mind reading demonstration, I often say, "I know what some of you are thinking right now…so, where's his hair?" This is a silly joke, but its purpose isn't only to get a laugh. Its purpose is for me to acknowledge the fact that I'm bald so that the audience can let it go and I can move on with the presentation. Not calling attention to something unusual about yourself or about a situation can leave the audience focusing on it throughout your entire speech. By simply calling it out yourself, you immediately eliminate it as a barrier between you and the audience.

Chew Gum

Chewing gum before you speak will help in a couple of ways. It keeps your mouth moistened; it relaxes your jaw muscles, and keeps your breath fresh. Why is fresh breath important? Well, anything that keeps your self-confidence high while onstage is worth doing, right? Plus, if someone is going to be using the microphone after you, you don't want it smell strange to him or her. I've had to use microphones after other speakers and I had to keep myself from yacking every time it came a bit too close to my nose! If you are chewing gum backstage, do not forget to get rid of it before stepping on stage. There are also some throat sprays, specifically designed for singers and speakers that will keep you vocal cords running smoothly. The one that I use is called Entertainer's Secret Throat Relief Spray and can be found on Amazon or at **entertainers-secret.com**.

Music

If you ever watch professional athletes, you'll notice that many, or even most, listen to music in their headphones when getting ready to compete. They do this to help get them into the "zone" and you can do the same. Just create a playlist with music that is sure to get you into a great mood and listen to it while backstage. I like to listen while I'm juggling. I find that the combination of good music and having to focus on catching five balls keeps my mind far too occupied to become worried about my upcoming speech.

Dress For Success

When deciding what to wear for your speech, a good rule of thumb is to dress slightly better than everyone else in the room, but not too much better. You want to look as though you have somewhere just a bit more important to be. Just don't over do it. You wouldn't want to wear a tuxedo to an event where the entire audience is in jeans. If the event you're speaking at requires attendees to wear nametags or convention badges, be sure to take yours off before going onstage. Wearing your nametag while speaking makes you look like an audience member who decided to get up and talk. Plus, it screams "Rookie!" You are the speaker, which makes you important, so ditch the name tag.

Using Your Instrument

Body Language

How you move onstage is important because the audience will subconsciously be reading your body language. If you've ever studied acting, you'll know that an actor predetermines every single movement of their body during a scene. Never make a gesture, expression, or movement without intention. If you're moving, there should be a reason for it. Even if that reason exists only in your mind. Unsure movements and gestures will convey a lack of confidence to the audience. I recommend that you do not stand behind a podium. This can make for an impersonal speech and your audience may become bored. Instead, use the entire space of the stage. Motion will create interest and keep your viewers active. Many speakers make the mistake of speaking only to the center of the room. Giving attention to only the center aisles can leave the people on the ends disinterested. Make a few points while standing at the center of the stage, then walk to the right, or left side of the stage to make your next point. This will continue to heighten their attention because it makes your speech feel more personalized, organic and alive.

It helps to make eye contact with the audience. Choose one person who looks unthreatening to you, and speak directly to them for a brief period of time. Then move onto someone else. This will help your speech come across as being more sincere. If you're afraid to make eye contact, you can fake it by looking just over the audience's heads, or by looking directly at a spot where no one is sitting. From the audience's point of view, it will look as though you're looking at the audience. Unless you have a specific reason for it, never put your hands in your pockets. Keep one hand on the microphone and use the other for gestures. When not gesturing, just allow that hand to swing naturally at your side.

Be Heard

It is more important to be heard than it is to be seen. Experiments have shown that people will watch a movie that has good sound, but crappy video quality. But, they will not watch a movie that has great video quality but crappy sound. Being heard is vital if you want to appear as a confident speaker. Don't be afraid to speak loud and clear. It's better to be a little bit too loud than to be a little bit too quiet. Being quiet shows weakness, but being loud shows confidence. Your aim is to speak loudly enough that the people in the back of the room can clearly hear you. When speakers are nervous, they tend to speed up their presentation a lot. I've seen speakers blast through, what was supposed to be a 60-minute speech, in 30-minutes! Don't forget to breathe, take pauses, and slow the heck down. I recommend taking a voice class. In a voice class, you will learn how to speak from your diaphragm, which will allow you to speak much more clearly and will enable you to project your voice into the largest of auditoriums. When technology fails and your microphone stops working, you'll still be able to be heard.

Microphone Technique

Most people assume that using a handheld microphone is as simple as holding it and talking. However, if you've ever been to an event where the audience starts shouting, "We can't hear you!" you know that this isn't the case. There are right and wrong ways to properly use a microphone. Step one is to understand that you need to talk over the top, or into the top of the microphone, not the side. Step two is to realize that you still need to talk at a normal, or above normal, volume level. Step three is to understand where to hold the microphone in conjunction to your mouth. Many beginners will begin holding the microphone about a foot below their chin. Then, as they continue to speak, they gradually lower the mic until it's almost at waist level, which means that they're getting quieter and quieter over time. This is a telltale sign of an amateur speaker.

Another beginner mistake is to begin gesturing with the hand that's holding the mic. This causes the volume of your voice to unrhythmically fade in and out and sounds terrible. The correct way to use most handheld microphones is to hold it so that the top of the mic is pointed towards your mouth at about a 45-degree angle. You don't want to speak directly into the top of the mic when it's close to your mouth or your "P" and "B" sounds will pop too much. The perfect distance will vary depending on the actual microphone, the sound levels, speaker position, and the layout of the room. It's always a good idea to have a sound check before your presentation prior to the audience's arrival.

If you find that your nerves are causing your hands to shake, and in turn causing the microphone to shake, there are simple remedies for that. First, don't hold the microphone at the bottom of the handle. Holding it too low will cause your hand shakes to be magnified at the top of the mic. Instead, keep your hand up higher, closer to the grill, or mesh-metal part of the mic. Don't go too high up to where your hand is cupping the grill unless you're a rapper. Keep about an inch of black showing between your hand and the grill. To keep the mic from shaking, simply press the side of the microphone's grill gently against the front-bottom of your chin. This will give you an anchor point to keep the microphone steady, and will also have it in a position so that you're speaking directly over the top of the grill. Try this out during your sound check first so that you can adjust your speaking volume levels accordingly. Because this technique puts the microphone very close to your mouth, you won't want to speak quite as loud.

Other Types of Microphones

Some venues will supply you with either a lavaliere, or clip-on microphone, or a headset mic. In these situations, allow the sound technician in the venue to properly set up the mic for you. They will know the ideal placement for the best quality sound. Just be sure, when using a lavalier that you don't have clothing that will brush against the mic or it will produce a nasty sound for the audience. You'll also want to avoid doing any hand gestures that will come in contact with the mic as this also sounds awful when the mic is live.

For more tips, tricks, techniques, and videos on becoming a powerful and confident speaker, visit www.CrushStageFright.com.

16 TAKE ACTION

Action is the real measure of intelligence.
- Napoleon Hill

Knowledge without application is like a book that is
never read. - Christopher Crawford

The Final Step

Everything that we've discussed so far will mean nothing if you don't take action on it. How many times have you read a book, attended a seminar, or learned a success secret, only to quickly move onto the next lesson before actually applying what you learned? I'm guilty of doing the same, but nothing great in my life has come from inaction. Stop being a collector of ideas and instead become a leader who follows through. The techniques in this book can only predict your destiny if they are applied, practiced, and perfected. It's too easy to fall into a cycle of never-ending preparation. With the principles that you have at your fingertips, you are ready to transform your dreams into your reality. Let's put this to work so that you can predict your own destiny and start living the life of your dreams.

In the chapter on intuition, we talked about how important it is to take action on the ideas supplied by your subconscious mind. It is equally as important that you take conscious actions without intuition as well. The more conscious actions you take toward achieving your planned destiny, the more active your subconscious mind will become. If you choose to skip out on actually filling out the workbook, practicing daily visualization, and utilizing self-hypnosis, then your success will be stunted.

This is not a system where you can pick and choose only the techniques that you "feel" might work for you. This system works because the whole is greater than the sum of the parts. You must utilize every technique in this book in order to slingshot your life into the direction of your planned destiny. Sure, you might have a degree of success by using only a few of the techniques, but that's not what this book is about. That is not why you're here. It is about you becoming the best possible version of you, and reaching your ultimate destiny. Attaining your planned destiny will provide yourself, your family, and those who follow you, an abundance of wealth, happiness, and fulfillment.

Make a promise to yourself right now, to commit to this system, wholeheartedly, for the next three months. If you do that, I guarantee that you will be amazed at what you're able to accomplish. After three months, these techniques will become habits, and you will be on the shortest route to becoming the ultimate leader and achiever that you can become.

The first conscious step to take is to make an action plan. Once you know where you want to end up, or your ultimate destiny, you must physically write down a plan that will get you there. The workbook, which is at the end of this book or online at **www.LeadershipMindPower.com/Workbook**, will make this process easy. Don't worry about creating a "The Perfect" plan, because that doesn't exist. Your plan will be an organic, ever-changing plan that must be flexible. As you go through the process of achieving your planned destiny, your plan to get there will change. Your subconscious mind will consistently deliver new, better, and faster ways to improve your plan, but it's vital that you start with a foundation plan in order for that to occur.

The best time to plant a tree was 20 years ago. The second best time is now. - Chinese Proverb

One of my favorite entrepreneurs, authors, influencers, and speakers is Gary Vaynerchuk. I've heard him say thousands of impactful things, but the most powerful thing that he's ever said, in my opinion, only used two words. He was ranting in one of his video blogs about the fact that so many people keep asking him the wrong questions. They want to know the best lighting to use when shooting video, the best microphones to use, and exactly what to say when posting social media content. These people want everything to be perfect before they begin. Gary's answer to this problem was simply, "Just start." Boom! Let that sink in. Write it down and post it everywhere, because it's huge. Make this your motto and never allow yourself to procrastinate again. Even on days when you don't feel like taking action, do it anyway. How you FEEL does NOT matter. You're going to feel much worse if you don't take action, so DO IT ANYWAY. I can promise that you're going to feel much better afterwards if you do it than if you don't. The key to reaching your destiny is to "Just start." That is the ONLY way to set all of this into motion! If you find yourself being stuck in a state of procrastination, check out my "Procrastination Deactivation" hypnosis program available at www.LiveHypnotist.com under the products tab.

Either you run the day or the day runs you. - Jim Rohn

Your Daily Action Plan

Now that you have your action plan in place, it's time to make sure you follow it relentlessly. The easiest and most effective way to do this is to plan your day, the night before, every night. At the end of each day, take a moment to reflect on the things that you've accomplished. Think about the things that went well and the things that could have gone better. Then write down, or use one of the many available apps, to plan your next day down to the minute. When doing this, it's important to focus on the tasks that are most vital to your destiny achieving success. Most likely, the things on your list that will make you feel the most uncomfortable are the ones that are most important and should be completed first. After you get those out of the way, you will have created incredible positive momentum for the rest of your day.

Your daily action list might start with waking up and reading your affirmations. That will get you into the right mindset to achieve your goals from the get-go, and will also remind you why you're doing what you're about to be doing. It will get your conscious mind focused and will also activate your subconscious mind. When writing your list, be sure to include the exact time frames allotted for each activity. This will keep you from putting off necessary tasks and will also encourage you to get more done in a shorter period of time.

After your affirmations, I recommend some form of exercise. You will want to start off your day with an intense feeling of positive emotion. Remember that your emotion is connected to your physical motion, so get moving. Even if your actual daily workout routine isn't scheduled until the evening, it's still important to do at least some form of movement in the morning. You could even do something as simple as 100 jumping jacks, some light stretching, or take a quick walk. I like to take a short 25-minute walk with my dogs each morning while listening to motivational music that I've edited together with my affirmations. It's amazing how much this will get you both physically and emotionally ready to conquer the day, plus my dogs love it too.

Don't make your entire daily action list about business. Be sure to also include time-slots for personal and family time. It's easy to become so obsessed with success that you begin to neglect other areas of your life. Without a happy family, your success will become meaningless. You don't want to reach your destiny only to find that you've lost touch with all of the other areas of your life. Including them in your action plan will guarantee them the time that they need and deserve. Adding something to your list as simple as, "Call and talk to Mom for

20-minutes," will keep you healthy, happy and sane. Plus, just think how special Mom will feel knowing that time dedicated to her is a part of your master plan!

As a leader, in order to keep your focus on the things that are most important for you to handle yourself, you will want to either delegate or outsource any tasks that don't require your personal skill-set. Time is the one thing that we don't have enough of, and the only way to create more time is to think of ourselves as corporations. It would be impossible for the CEO of a corporation to run all aspects of the business. Never think that you must achieve your destiny alone. Build a team around yourself, whether it's through mentors, friends, employees, or through outsourcing, to help you achieve far more in a shorter period of time than you ever could alone. With websites like Fiverr.com, Upwork.com, eLance.com, etc., finding people to tackle tasks is both inexpensive and effective. With these sites, you can have others working to help you achieve your destiny even while you're asleep. Talk about adding time to your quest. This is a no-brainer.

The problem that I see with many is that they're afraid to hand over, even the most mundane tasks, to others because they don't trust that anyone else can do it as well as they can. If that thought crosses your mind, just remember that your work doesn't have to always be perfect. What's important is that it gets done. Speed of implementation is often the key, especially when acting on information given to you from your subconscious mind. Rather than put a task off until you have enough extra time to do it, outsource it and get it done today. George Patton said, "A good plan violently executed now is better than a perfect plan executed next week." So, "Just start!" Thanks again #AskGaryVee!

Never confuse motion with action. - Ben Franklin

Busy Work And The 80/20 Rule

There's a very big difference between being busy and being productive. Being busy doesn't cut it. Busy people are broke. When you decide what daily actions you're going to take, it's imperative that your chosen actions are the ones that will actually move you closer towards the achievement of your planned destiny. It's very easy to find yourself hiding behind "busy" work in an attempt to avoid more important tasks. Often, the reason for this is that the most important tasks tend to be the ones that require you to step out of your comfort zone.

If you have trouble distinguishing between busy work and vital work, which most of us do, the Pareto principle is an excellent resource to implement into your plan. The Pareto principle or better known as the 80/20 Rule implies that 20% of our actions produce 80% of our results. Once you're able to pinpoint which 20% of your actions produce your greatest results, those are the ones to focus on. The other 80% of your necessary actions can either be saved for another time or outsourced. Most of the time, your 20% will be the things that require you to step out of your comfort zone the furthest. Why? Because those are the steps that few are willing to take, and that's why so many people are never able to reach their full potential. But, if you're able to identify your 20%, and commit to taking action on them by adding them to your daily action plan, you are going to produce results to the like that most will never experience.

While Pareto's principle states the equation to be 80/20, don't feel stuck to fulfilling 20% of your needed activities. Some will find that 5% of their actions yield 95% of their outcome. If that's the case, focus on that 5% and outsource the rest. Do whatever it is that produces the greatest, and fastest results towards the attainment of your destiny. The 80/20 Rule does not only apply to the attainment of your financial success, but also to your health, relationships, and happiness.

I should mention a distinct difference, when referencing outsourcing, between activities that lie within your inner genius, activities that require you to step out of your comfort zone, and activities that you simply aren't good at. Just because an action step requires you to step out of your comfort zone is not an excuse to outsource it. As mentioned previously, those are often the most important steps to your success, and handling those types of actions off to others could thwart your progress. But, if an action step falls into the 80% category, especially if it's not within your inner genius, then you should certainly seek to outsource it. Avoid taking on actions that you simply do not enjoy doing, unless they're in the 20% category. If you don't enjoy doing them but find that they're in the 20%, those are the actions that should be completed by you first and foremost each day.

17 PERSISTENCE

Nothing in this world can take the place of persistence.
Talent will not. Nothing is more common than
unsuccessful men with talent. Genius will not.
Unrewarded genius is almost a proverb. Education will
not. The world is full of educated derelicts. Persistence
and determination alone are omnipotent.
- Calvin Coolidge

Fighting Resistance With Perseverance

Along your journey towards the fulfillment of your planned destiny, one thing is certain. You will absolutely be confronted with resistance. The only way to push through resistance is with persistence and willpower. Without an attitude of persistence, you will likely give up on your dreams before they ever have a chance to create momentum. Resistance might come from many places and in many forms. These include your friends, family, and coworkers, but it will certainly come from you as well. Utilizing The Law of Attraction requires a reprogramming of the subconscious mind, and as you now know, the subconscious mind resists change. Most of the people, who have applied the success principles taught throughout this book, who claim, "That stuff just doesn't work," are the ones who gave in to resistance. They stopped trying before they were able to reach the tipping point of success. They gave up before they pushed their boulder over the hill, and they allowed it to roll back down and crush their ambition. They were not persistent, or at least, not persistent enough.

Whenever you feel uncomfortable, instead of retreating
back into your old comfort zone, pat yourself on the
back and say, 'I must be growing,' and continue
moving forward. - T. Harv Eker

In "Think & Grow Rich," Napoleon Hill writes about persistence, "The majority of people are ready to throw their aims and purposes overboard, and give up at the first sign of opposition or misfortune. A few carry on DESPITE all opposition, until they attain their goal." The good news is that persistence is an attribute that can be obtained by anyone who truly desires to reach his or her destiny. If you only "kind of" want it, then resistance will likely stop you in your tracks. That's why it's so important to choose a destiny that you're truly passionate about, and that you have a burning desire to manifest.

An excellent tool to help you acquire persistence is accountability. Hill recommends forming, or joining a mastermind group. You could also find a mentor, coach, or friend to help keep you accountable. Then, when resistance rears its ugly head, your mastermind group or coach can help motivate you to keep pushing forward. They will remind you that resistance is inevitable and of the benefits that pushing through will bring.

Whenever you feel like giving up, remind yourself that there is no such thing as failure. Failure only exists in your mind. At best, the only power that failures have is postponing your success. Hill wrote that, "Most great people have attained their greatest success just one step beyond their greatest failure." With this in your heart, failure is not something to be feared. It is evidence that you're getting closer to achieving something great. Eventually, you WILL arrive and look back on temporary failures as needed stepping stones that led you to where you ultimately needed to be. They will have been temporary setbacks that eventually led you, even if somewhat indirectly, to your planned destiny.

Believe it or not, successful people have bad days, too.
The difference is they don't let their feelings dictate
their actions. - Lewis Howes

Pushing Through Is Key

When things don't seem to be going exactly as you had envisioned in your mind, you must force yourself to continue to follow through with your daily actions. Your resistance might be so powerful that you will occasionally lose your will to battle on, but that's why we have been working so hard to turn your daily actions into habits. Remember that how you "feel" does not matter. You must find a way to take the actions anyway. What you are feeling at these moments are only slumps. It is your subconscious mind fighting to remain unchanged. It's a completely natural feeling and must be pushed through if you are to reach the next level of success. And, keep in mind, that pushing through these moments of doubt, and resistance, will enable you to reach even higher levels of success in the future. It's as though your subconscious mind is getting to the next level of a video game. Each level might become more difficult, but if you're able to conquer your current level, it will allow you to challenge more advanced levels that carry with them much larger rewards.

You may be tempted to stop using daily visualization, affirmations, and hypnosis after a while. That happens because, while these actions are easy to adopt, they do take up time. Do not make this mistake. The key to making this system work is daily, continuous, massive action. Even if it feels as though your subconscious mind has accepted your suggestions about becoming the person you intend to be, you must not let up. You need to finish off those old beliefs about yourself or they will come back to haunt you. Have you ever seen a horror movie where the star has a chance to kill the monster, but chooses not to? For some reason, they think that simply wounding the monster will be enough, but what always happens next? Exactly. The monster comes back, kills more people, and sequels are made. Don't allow your subconscious mind to make a sequel of the old you. Complete the process of becoming the new, more powerful, more responsible, more effective, more successful, you. To do this, you must continue with your daily actions until you have physically become the person that you had intended to become. It takes time for your subconscious mind to COMPLETELY accept positive change. Zig Ziglar said, "People often say that motivation doesn't last. Well, neither does bathing - that's why we recommend it daily." As silly, or as time consuming as it may seem, you must continue to overwhelm your subconscious mind until it unconditionally adopts the new version of you. Do this until those thoughts have manifested themselves as your actual reality.

> Whatever the mind can conceive and BELIEVE,
> the mind can achieve. - Napoleon Hill

Believing In Yourself

The above quote is an important one. If you do not believe that you have the ability to achieve your planned destiny, then you will most likely not achieve it. The scary part is that what we believe is not a choice. We either believe something or we do not. You cannot "decide" to believe something. Sure, you can "say" that you believe something, but what matters is what you feel rather than speak.

For example, imagine that a terrorist is pointing a gun at your head. The masked gunman says that he's going to kill you and your entire family if you don't believe in his version of a god. In order not to offend anyone, let's say that his god is a mystical groundhog. A mystical groundhog, with five heads, that lives hidden inside a secret volcano on a distant planet. The terrorist says that you cannot simply "say" that you believe in his groundhog god, but that you must actually "believe" in it. In fact, he's going to hook you up to the world's most advanced lie detector system that no-one is able to beat. Could you do it? Most could probably not. That's because belief is not a decision. You either believe in something or you don't.

The good news is that our beliefs can change. No, I'm not saying that you can eventually believe in the groundhog god. I'm just saying that beliefs can and do change. In order to change what you believe, especially when it comes to what you believe about your potential, you must work to reprogram your thinking. Everything that we've covered so far in this book has all been designed to help you change your beliefs about yourself. You see, when your conscious and subconscious minds become congruent, you will begin to experience massive success. Massive success is evidence that you are becoming the person that you desire to become. Evidence is what is needed to change our beliefs and you will soon find that your belief in yourself to accomplish extraordinary tasks will begin to grow exponentially. That kind of belief carries with it massive amounts of power that can slingshot your success beyond moon.

It will certainly take persistence for all of this to have the momentum of an avalanche, but it WILL come. Most of the people who have applied this system to reaching their goals have seen their success grow on what is called a hockey stick curve. For a while, at least for many, the progress is gradual. This period is like the blade of the hockey stick. But then, all of a sudden, things will take a major upward curve and continue to grow to the point of reaching your destiny, or in many cases, shooting far past the point of your original goal. Don't expect everything to happen right at the beginning. Focus on putting in the work, and soon enough, you will reap the rewards.

18 THE POWER OF GRATITUDE

> ...Gratitude is the antidote to the things that mess us up. You can't be angry and grateful simultaneously. You can't be fearful and grateful simultaneously. So, gratitude is the solution to both anger and fear... - Tony Robbins

Gratitude

What is the one thing that will stop most people from actually applying the principles from this book towards the achievement of their destinies? The answer is inaction caused by fear. Fear, which comes from an improper programming of our subconscious minds, can be so overwhelming for some that they will never even take the first step, let alone push through until the end. So what does fear have to do with gratitude? This is a concept that I learned from Tony Robbins. Robbins said that, "Fear cannot exist in a state of gratitude." I confess that the first time I heard that statement, it didn't click. I didn't understand what gratitude had to do with success. That was until I tested what Robbins had said, and he was right. I know it sounds strange, but give the exercise below a try and see what you experience.

An Exercise In Gratitude:

Take a break from reading, find a nice quiet spot, and plan to sit down for several minutes. Begin by taking some nice, slow, deep, breaths as you begin to relax your body. Close your eyes, and start to think about everything in your life that you are honestly grateful for. Examples include: Your health, your family members, your friends, your house, car, the books that have inspired you, the actors who made your favorite movie, your pets, etc. Don't just think of these items as a list. Go through each one, one at a time, and allow yourself to experience the emotions that arise while you're saying to yourself, and to the people on your list, and/or the universe, or the God of your belief, "Thank you so much for putting this in my life" or, something along those lines. Whatever phrase brings about the most emotion for you is best. Then imagine giving them a big thank you hug and let those positive emotions fill your body and mind completely.

Did you happen to notice during the exercise that the thought of fear was nowhere to be found? If fear did happen to slip into your thoughts, it only happened during a moment when gratitude slipped away. Like meditation, this exercise will require practice. If you find your mind slipping onto other thoughts that have nothing to do with gratitude, just make a mental note of it, and then slowly steer your mind back to gratitude. Whenever I find myself falling into a phase of un-motivation, I immediately stop what I'm doing and go into this exercise. Sometimes, if I'm not able to find a quiet space, I'll do it while driving or just before making an important phone call. It's amazing how much this simple practice of conscious gratitude can change your life. You will find that you are more appreciative of the people and things around you, and those around you will notice a difference as well.

Being in a state of gratitude is also a powerful tool to use when attempting something that might normally cause you to feel fear or anxiety. For example, if you're about to make an important sales call, but find yourself feeling nervous, you can use gratitude to completely transform your feelings. Instead of asking yourself, "What if I screw this up?" Or, "What if they don't like me?" Change your thought to one of gratitude. Be thankful that you have the opportunity to call this person up and provide them with something that will make his or her life easier. Think about how grateful you're going to be when they say, "Yes!" Then, be sure to feel the emotions that will come along with that answer. Once you're feeling powerful, grateful, and positive, pick up the phone and make the call. Simply by taking an action with a preempted feeling of gratitude towards the end result, will make taking that action a pleasure for you instead of a pain.

19 HOW TO IMPLEMENT EVERYTHING

One of the things that I've struggled with over the years is information overload. How is it possible to make sure that you implement all of your favorite techniques and lessons from the hundreds of books, video courses, and coaches that inspire you in a lifetime? I like to go back and reread books that have had powerful impacts on my life. Every time I do this, I find ideas that I had forgotten about. Ideas that, when I first read them, I had planned on plugging in to my own life system. But, because of the sheer volume of useful information, I had completely forgotten about some of the best ideas. I'll be re-reading a book and think, "Oh my God, if only I had been applying this all along, where would I be today?" So, I've come up with a system that allows me to immediately implement every idea that I want into my life. And, the ideas don't get accidentally abandoned over the course of a few weeks.

What I do is take notes on every book that I read, every seminar that I attend, and every idea that I learn from my coaches. I then go through the notes and highlight each idea that I want to make certain not to forget. Next, I list the ideas onto a piece of paper and record myself saying them one by one. I record them in the positive. For example, if an idea is that I want to practice getting into a state of gratitude every day, I'll record myself saying, "I get into a state of gratitude every single day." I then edit this recording into my daily affirmations and visualization track that I listen to when doing my morning walk. Yes, you'll have to edit this from time to time, but it becomes a daily reminder of all of the things you want to implement into your life. I'll also listen to my recording while falling asleep on an airplane. This might sound like a lot of effort to remember to utilize new knowledge, but being able to actually apply every useful thing that you learn into your life will allow you to grow as a person at lightning speed.

If you'd like to make your own recording, but don't feel that you are tech-savvy, don't worry because it's very simple. All you have to do is record it using your smartphone voice recorder app. Then import the recording into an audio, or even video, editing software like iMovie, Final Cut Pro, or the free audio editing software Audacity. Those will allow you to edit the recording and even mix in some music in the background. I find that, at the end of my daily run or walk, I am completely recharged and motivated to take massive action. You can do the same with your daily affirmations and visualizations. Everything can be edited together into one single track that you can listen to daily or anytime you need a good boost of confidence. And, the longer your list becomes, the more exercise you end up getting and that's a good thing.

20 NETWORKING 101

Throughout your journey to achieving your predetermined destiny, you're going to need the cooperation and the help of others. Your tribe will assist you so that you don't have to do any of this alone. You will build your tribe through leadership, public speaking, and networking. Below are 10 effective ways to stand out from the crowd when networking. Applying these 10 networking principles will accelerate your efforts towards surrounding yourself with a team of people who serve as your allies along the way.

1. Be memorable

People tend to remember things much better when they're visual, so make it easy for them. Memory experts will often link a word or an image to something else in order to help them remember it. When you introduce yourself, try to provide a visualization of yourself. For example, if your name is Donald and you're bald, you could say something like, "Hi, my name is Donald. Just picture Donald Trump with a shaved head. Do you see it?" Now sure, that's a silly example, but when it comes to remembering, silly is a good thing. I guarantee that they will always remember the bald Donald. Create a unique visualization for your name and stick to it.

2. Remember Their Names

How many times have you had someone, who you can't quite remember, come up to you and say, "Hello Chad, nice to see you again?" Do you remember the impact it had on you? We're always impressed when someone remembers our name. It makes us feel special, and that person rises up a few notches on our respectability scale. In order to easily remember someone's name, first say the person's name a few times out loud. Not in a creepy way, but incorporate their name into the conversation. This will make them feel important and get the name to stick in your mind. The most effective way to get their name into your long term memory, using this technique, is to say it once, wait a minute, say it again, wait 3 minutes, say it again, wait 5 minutes, and so on. Eventually, it will be locked into your permanent, long-term memory.

Again, people tend to remember things much better when they're visual, so try to link their name to something that it either sounds like or reminds you of. Then, find a unique facial feature about that person, or anything else that immediately stands out when you look at them. Exaggerate it in your mind, and make it interact, in an interesting way, with your visualized word. For example, if the person has incredibly blue eyes, you might imagine that their eyes are made of laser-beam-shooting crystals. If their name is Mike, it might make you think of a microphone. Then you might imagine that person walking into a conference room and blowing up all of the microphones with his blue laser beam eyes. The next time you see his blue eyes, you'll immediately remember Mike's name. Just remember to make your visualization as vivid and wild as possible. You must see the event in your mind as though you were actually there in order for this to work. With practice, this technique will only take a second or two, but the memory will last forever.

3. Make Your Name Tag Unique

If wearing a nametag, as we do at most networking events, you'll want to make sure yours stands out. Don't just put down your name, company, and job title. That's just boring! For this, take a lesson from network marketing companies who wear buttons that say something like, "Ask me how I can make you rich." Is that a better conversation starter than, "My name is Bob?" You bet it is! Don't just copy that one though. It's old-hat. Get creative! Try to incorporate your own USP (Unique Selling Proposition). What problem is it that your product or service can solve for people? That's what you want to use. And, if you have a good sense of humor, now's the time to use it. Just like a speech, it's always better to start a conversation with a laugh when possible. Just be sure to keep the humor clean and non-political.

4. Don't just hand out you business cards

Sure handing out your card is fine, but you must collect theirs too. You'll want to save the business card exchange for later in the conversation. Don't hand out your card as your introduction. That can feel forced and needy. Instead, look to make a connection with the person and start a relationship. Exchange cards AFTER you find commonalities and ways that you might be able to benefit each other. When accepting a business card, be sure to look at the card for a moment, actually read it, and be interested in it. Then put it safely in a special place. Don't just jam it into your pocket of forgetfulness. Show them that you care by placing their card in a special place, perhaps in your wallet.

5. Listen when they speak

We've already dedicated an entire chapter to the power of listening, but it bears repeating. If you don't seem interested in them, then they certainly won't be interested in you. How many times have you met someone at a networking event, and while you're talking, you notice that they seem more interested in what's going on across the room? Please, don't be that person! Ever! When you first meet someone, the best thing that you can do is ask questions, and then listen…I mean REALLY listen to their answers. Avoid questions that can be answered with a simple yes or no. Go for questions that will allow them to brag a little bit. They'll be surprised that you're interested, and will be honored to share their stories. In a word full of me-mongers, this simple step can really make you stand out and be remembered.

6. Allow the Focus to Be on Them

Focus on what you can do for them, and NOT what they can do for you. As soon as you begin to talk about YOU, you've lost them. Allow the conversation to go where THEY choose. Be, don't act, interested. Ask questions and find out if there's a way for you to help them. Can you, or someone in your network, solve one of their problems? Don't worry; eventually, maybe not even today, you'll get your chance to share how awesome YOU are. People tend to hire and work with people whom they know, like, and trust, and if you become a problem solver for them, you will earn their trust and be very well liked.

7. Be Creative With Your Contact Info

Don't have a boring old business card. Honestly, how many stacks of business cards do you have at home right now, stuffed into a junk drawer? That's because they're all the same. Cards that are the same size, same shape, same weight, etc. are like a pile of camouflage. So, what can we do to save our cards from the "junk drawer of doom?"

Here are a few ideas:

- People tend to treat cards with a person's photo with more respect, so consider adding your photo to your card
- Cards in a stack can be forgotten, so don't make your card stackable.
- Try using a tent-style business card, or a uniquely shaped card.
- Consider not using a business card at all. Instead, carry a stack of business postcards or flyers with you

8. Make Your Elevator Pitch Fun!

Never go unprepared to a networking event. You should arrive with a purpose. Know ahead of time who you'd like to meet and why. Plan exactly what you're going to say when someone asks about your product or services. Your elevator pitch, since it should be pre-written, can and SHOULD be both interesting and entertaining. If you want to be remembered, think of your pitch as a very short infomercial. Never focus on the feature of your products or services. Instead, ALL of the focus should be on how your products or services can BENEFIT others. Never state a feature, unless you immediately follow up the benefit of that feature. Since your elevator pitch is something that you'll use over and over again, take enough time to make it good. Try to incorporate humor when appropriate, be visual and act confident. If script writing isn't your thing, consider outsourcing it. The chapter on public speaking will help with this as well.

9. Don't Forget To Brush Your Teeth

Yes, this sounds silly and obvious, but nothing throws off an introduction like spinach in your teeth! Check our teeth, check your breath, and make sure your didn't forget to put on deodorant in the morning. First impressions are everything, and bad hygiene is an instant social FAIL. Once you know your teeth are clean, don't forget to smile. People who smile are TWICE as likely to be remembered!

10. Keep A Database Of Your Networking Contacts

Finally, if you have 500+ contacts on LinkedIn, it can be nearly impossible to keep track of who's who. Do yourself a favor and create a Google spreadsheet or a CRM (Customer Relationship Management) program to keep your networking contacts organized. Jot down notes about each person. What they do, what they're interested in, what their favorite sports teams are, etc. These may come in very handy in the future. Once you've made your connections, you must follow up. Without following up, networking is pointless. Pick up the phone, connect on LinkedIn, Facebook, or send an email. If ever you're able to solve a problem for someone in your new network, do it. Even if doing so doesn't make you any money at the time. Connecting once isn't enough. Keep the conversations going and build relationships. That's what networking is all about anyway, right?

CONCLUSION

We've come to the end of the book, but just the beginning of your journey. I'd like to leave you with a few final thoughts that I feel are important. The first is why many readers will simply put this book down without ever taking an action step. They'll say, "Cool, I finished another book. Yeah for me! Now, what should I read next?" They'll do this without applying what they've learned as many of us perpetual readers do. Please do not let that be you. It's time to stop learning and to start achieving. Put your money where your mouth is and take some freaking action!

Don't be afraid to suck

One of the reasons that people will never take even the first step towards achieving their destinies is because they're afraid to suck. Coming from an entertainment background, I can completely relate to this. In order to become a great magician, you must first be willing to be a lousy magician. This holds true for pretty much any endeavor. The ONLY way to become competent at any skill, is to first be willing to suck. Why? Sticking to the magician analogy, mastery of entertainment, or any new undertaking, only happens through experience. When talking to young magicians, I'm often asked, "But, what do I do if a trick goes wrong or if someone heckles me?" My answer is that it's going to suck...at least at first, but that's a good thing. You need to put yourself into high-pressure situations so that you can learn how to handle them yourself. With experience, you will develop your character and create personal systems for handling these situations.

When I wanted to become a professional level magician, I began to perform at every possible situation that came my way. I wanted to put myself into situations that would make me feel as nervous and uncomfortable as possible. I knew that if I could overcome those obstacles, everything else would be easy. A great example was when I received a phone call from a local comedy club that I had performed at. The club owner had been contacted by the owner of an exotic dance club who had decided that he wanted to have a comedy-night once per month. I needed the money, and the experience, so I took the gig. I showed up to the dingiest of bars in a scary part of town and unloaded my props. When I walked into the club, I saw that it was filled with completely nude women who were being gawked at by what I can only describe as a bunch of redneck men who looked like part of a biker gang. My instinct was to turn around and walk right out of that club, but I reminded myself that this experience will only make me a better performer…even if I sucked. Here's where it got crazy. The DJ killed the music, came over the public announcement system and screamed, "All right, ladies, go ahead and get dressed. It's time for the magic show!" EVERYONE in the club booed and hissed, especially when they realized that the magician was me and not one of the girls! I thought that I was about to have my ass kicked.

It took me about ten minutes to finally win over the crowd, but somehow I did. It went so well that the owner invited me back again the following month. Now, this certainly wasn't my finest moment in show business, but it irrefutably raised my level of courage. If I could win over a bunch of drunken bikers who had zero interest in seeing my show, then I could certainly handle anything that a corporate audience could throw at me. It would have been so easy for me to turn down the gig, but turning it down wouldn't have given me a venue to risk failure. Performing time and again in, less than ideal, situations turned me into the confident performer that I am today. The point that I'm trying to get across is that you cannot be afraid to suck. Not only that, but the faster you're willing to suck, the better. If you wait until the perfect moment to take action, it will never happen. Get started right now and, in time you will look back and wonder how you came so far. It drives me crazy when would-be speakers say, "Well, I'm not as confident onstage as you are." That's because I wasn't afraid to suck. So suck it up and start sucking today! Capish?

Some thoughts on happiness

I will leave you with a few thoughts on happiness. Achieving your ultimate destiny will certainly bring about a temporary feeling of happiness, but you must not allow your happiness to depend completely upon the fulfillment of your plan. To do so can be dangerous to your well-being. The time to feel happy is not upon the completion of your goal, but throughout the entire process. Many people get stuck in the belief that they'd be happy if only a certain event occurred. Then, when that one certain thing does happen, they quickly realize that the feeling of happiness is fleeting or temporary. Happiness is not something to strive for, it is something that you simply are. It is not something for the future nor something of the past. Happiness is for right now. You must DECIDE to be happy daily.

To better explain what I mean, I want you to think back to something that you really wanted in your life that eventually occurred. Perhaps, it was buying a certain car that you wanted, or getting that promotion that you wanted. You probably felt happy about that event for a few days, or maybe even for a few months, but did it last? Did it keep you happy forever? It probably did not. That's because true happiness is not found in the achievement of a goal, but in the quest to achieve it. As long as you choose a destiny that really means something to you, and as long as you choose something that lies within your inner genius, you will find happiness along the way, all the way up to its fruition and beyond.

Another way to view this concept of perpetual happiness is by looking at music, movies and stories. The philosopher, Alan Watts said,

"The meaning and purpose of dancing is the dance. Like music, also, it is fulfilled in each moment of its course. You do not play a sonata in order to reach the final chord, and if the meanings of things were simply in ends, composers would write nothing but finales."

If you apply the principles taught throughout this book, I am confident that you will achieve any destiny that you desire. But, even if you don't, the growth and fulfillment that you will experience in your life will far outweigh the life that you would've had without it.

You are much more capable than you know. Begin today to unleash your full potential. I promise that you will astound yourself by what you are able to accomplish. Choose your destiny wisely by staying within your inner genius. The path will take you to a place that you didn't even know existed. It will take you to a place far beyond your imagination. When you get there, please, let me know. I would love to hear from you and would be honored to be of service in any way that I'm able. Thank you so much for reading my book and I wish you the best of success and happiness in all of your ventures.

Awesome Resources To Keep You Fired Up

Below are some of the resources that will help keep you motivated along your journey. These include access to the workbooks mentioned throughout the book, newsletters, other books, podcasts, etc.

1. To access the free workbooks that go along with this book, visit **www.LeadershipMindPower.com/workbook.** All you have to do is enter your name and email address and you'll receive instant access. The reason we ask for your email address is so that we can keep track of who's accessing the materials, and also so that we can keep you up to date on changes and updates to the book. We'll also send emails from time to time, don't worry, we won't overdo it, that will be filled with valuable information to help you along the way. We despise spam and promise to never abuse your email. Just do us a favor and whitelist our email address after signing up, so that our messages don't end up in your spam folder.

2. The Crush Stage Fright ebook and Video Course. The purpose of Crush Stage Fright is to help you become the best public speaker that you can be. We will go into much greater detail on the topics of conquering stage fright and how to deliver powerful speaking presentations, complete with videos, articles, and tips that we didn't have time to cover in this book. It's awesome, so check it out.

www.CrushStageFright.com

3. Recommended Reading: Here is a list of books that I believe will have a major positive impact on your life:

In alphabetical order:

1. #AskGaryVee: One Entrepreneur's Take on Leadership, Social Media, and Self-Awareness by Gary Vaynerchuk
2. *Book Yourself Solid* by Michael Port
3. DOTCOM Secrets: The Underground Playbook For Growing Your Company Online by Russell Brunson
4. Expert Secrets by Russell Brunson
5. Fanatical Prospecting: The Ultimate Guide for Starting Sales Conversations and Filling the Pipeline by Leveraging Social Selling, Telephone, E-mail, and Cold Calling by Jeb Blount
6. Goals! How to Get Everything You Want Faster Than You Ever Thought Possible by Brian Tracy
7. How to Win Friends and Influence Others by Dale Carnegie
8. Leap First: Creating Work That Matters by Seth Godin
9. MONEY Master the Game by Tony Robbins
10. Never Split the Difference: Negotiating as if Your Life Depended on It by Chris Voss
11. Outwitting the Devil by Napoleon Hill
12. Pitch Anything: An Innovative Method for Presenting, Persuading, and Winning the Deal by Oren Klaff
13. Profit First: A Simple System to Transform Any Business from a Cash-Eating Monster to a Money-Making Machine by Mike Michalowicz
14. The 5 Second Rule: Transform Your Life, Work, and Confidence with Everyday Courage by Mel Robbins
15. The ABC's of Success: The Essential Principles From America's Greatest Prosperity Teacher by Bob Proctor
16. The Little Red Book of Selling: 12.5 Principles of Sales Greatness by Jeffrey Gitomer
17. The Power of Starting Something Stupid: How to Crush Fear, Make Dreams Happen, and Live Without Regret by Richie Norton

18. <u>The School of Greatness: A Real-World Guide to Living Bigger, Loving Deeper, and Leaving a Legacy</u> by Lewis Howes
19. <u>The Tipping Point: How Little Things Can Make a Big Difference</u> by Malcolm Gladwell
20. <u>The War of Art: Winning the Inner Creative Battle</u> by Steven Pressfield
21. <u>Think & Grow Rich</u> by Napoleon Hill
22. <u>Tools of Titans</u> by Tim Ferriss
23. <u>Tribes: We Need You to Lead Us</u> by Seth Godin
24. <u>You Were Born Rich: Now You Can Discover and Develop Those Riches</u> by Bob Proctor

4. Recommended Podcasts

The School of Greatness with Lewis Howes
The Tim Ferriss Show with Tim Ferriss
Sell or Die with Jeffrey Gitomer and Jennifer Gluckow
I Love Marketing with Joe Polish and Dean Jackson
The Tony Robbins Podcast
The GaryVee Audio Experience with Gary Vaynerchuk
Marketing in Your Car with Russell Brunson
Entrepreneur on Fire with John Lee Dumas

ABOUT THE AUTHOR

Chad Chesmark has been speaking on stages since he received his first magic kit at the age of six. By the age of eight, he was performing shows throughout his neighborhood. With the goal of becoming a better stage performer and speaker, Chad earned degrees in business and organizational communication, sociology, public relations, and theater arts. While attending university, he supplemented his income by speaking and performing at schools, comedy clubs and corporate events.

When he's not speaking about leadership and mental mastery, or performing on land, Chad spends time each year as a headlining entertainer for Royal Caribbean, Celebrity, Holland America, Princess, and Disney Cruise Lines. The high demand for Chad's presentations has enabled him to perform over 1,000 presentations across the globe, in front of more than a million audience members.

Chad became obsessed with the powers of the human mind after reading Napoleon Hill's, "Think and Grow Rich." That book changed his life and inspired him to become a certified stage hypnotist so that he could learn how to master the subconscious mind. His keynote talks incorporate this skill through the use of humor, visualization, and self-hypnosis. In his keynotes, he teaches the audience to literally update their mental software.

Chad's love of speaking, entertaining, and empowering others to achieve shines through in each performance, and his dedication to customizing each show for his clients keeps him in high demand. Whether he's speaking at a small sales meeting, large leadership conference, or attracting crowds on the trade show floor, Chad's programs are sure to leave a powerful, positive impression.

CONTACT INFORMATION

Download Workbook: www.LeadershipMindPower.com/workbook
Speaking Services: www.LeadershipMindPower.com
Entertainment Services: www.ChadChesmark.com
Trade Show Presenter Services: www.TheTradeShowGuy.com
Stage Hypnosis Presentations: www.LiveHypnotist.com
Crush Stage Fright Book & Video Course:
http://www.CrushStageFright.com

51838823R00092

Made in the USA
Lexington, KY
06 September 2019